Make Your Worrier a Warrior

A Guide to Conquering Your Child's Fears

by
Dan Peters, Ph.D.

Great Potential Press™

Make Your Worrier a Warrior: A Guide to Conquering Your Child's Fears

Edited by: Jennifer Ault
Interior design: The Printed Page
Cover design: Hutchison-Frey
All illustrations by Tracy Hill, © 2013

Published by Great Potential Press, Inc.
1325 N. Wilmot Road, Suite 300
Tucson, AZ 85712
www.greatpotentialpress.com

17 16 15 14 13   5 4 3 2 1

At the time of this book's publication, all facts and figures cited are the most current available. All telephone numbers, addresses, and website URLs are accurate and active; all publications, organizations, websites, and other resources exist as described in this book; and all have been verified as of the time this book went to press. The author(s) and Great Potential Press make no warranty or guarantee concerning the information and materials given out by organizations or content found at websites, and we are not responsible for any changes that occur after this book's publication. If you find an error or believe that a resource listed here is not as described, please contact Great Potential Press.

Great Potential Press provides a wide range of authors for speaking events. To find out more, go to www.greatpotentialpress.com/do-you-need-a-speaker, email info@greatpo-tentialpress.com, or call (520) 777-6161.

Library of Congress Cataloging-in-Publication Data

Peters, Daniel B., 1970-
  Make your worrier a warrior : a guide to conquering your child's fears /
Daniel B. Peters, Ph.D.
    pages cm
  Includes bibliographical references and index.
  ISBN-13: 978-1-935067-23-8 (pbk.)
  ISBN-10: 1-935067-23-0 (pbk.)
  1. Worry in children. 2. Anxiety in children. 3. Fear in children. I.
Title.
  BF723.W67P47 2014
  155.4'1246--dc23
2013029736

Dedication

For my wife,
Lizzie,
my partner in life and my greatest ally in fighting the monsters

Table of Contents

Acknowledgments   xi

Introduction   1
   So How Did I Become an Anxiety Expert?   1
   Why This Book?   4
   About This Book   6

Chapter 1. Who Is the Worry Monster?   9
   Some Examples of Worriers   9
   What if It Seems Your Child Doesn't Want to Be Helped? 12
   Creating Separation   13
   Pulling Back the Curtain   14
   Things to Remember   17
   Things to Do   18

Chapter 2. Anxiety and the Fear Response   19
   The Survival Response   20
   Things to Remember   27
   Things to Do   27

Chapter 3. Types of Anxiety and What They Look Like   29
   Generalized Anxiety   30
   Panic Attacks   30
   Agoraphobia   31
   Obsessive-Compulsive Disorder (OCD)   32
   Specific Phobia   33
   Social Phobia   34
   Post-Traumatic Stress Disorder (PTSD)   34
   Separation Anxiety   35
   Perfectionism   36

Eating Disorders   38

Time to Relax and Breathe   39

Activity: What Neighborhood Are We In?   40

What Does Anxiety Look Like?   42

Avoidance   43

Things to Remember   45

Things to Do   46

Neighborhood Activity Answers   46

Chapter 4. Cognitive Model of Anxiety   **47**

Thoughts Cause Feelings   47

How the Worry Monster Works   48

Here Comes Adrenaline!   50

Taking on the Worry Monster   51

Things to Remember   51

Things to Do   52

Chapter 5. Thinking Errors   **53**

Catastrophizing   54

All or Nothing Thinking   54

Filtering   54

Selective Attention   55

Magnifying   55

Shoulds   55

Mind Reading   56

Personalizing   56

Overgeneralizing   56

Probability Overestimation   57

Additional Thinking Errors   57

   "What if…?"   57

   "What will people think…?"   58

The Short List   58

Activity: What Are Your Child's (and Your) Thinking Patterns?   59

Things to Remember   60

Things to Do   60

Thinking Patterns Activity Answers   61

Chapter 6. Cognitive (Thinking) Interventions   63
  Four Steps   64
  Additional Cognitive Strategies   68
    Positive Self-Talk   68
    Worry Time   70
    Worry Box   71
    "And then what?"   71
    Planning for Worst-Case Scenarios   72
  Things to Remember   73
  Things to Do   74

Chapter 7. Mindfulness-Based Interventions   75
  Staying in the Present   76
  Letting Thoughts Pass   79
  Controlling Your Breathing   81
    Activity: Belly Breathing   82
  Things to Remember   84
  Things to Do   84

Chapter 8. Behavioral Interventions: Practice, Practice, Practice!   85
  Systematic Desensitization, Success Ladders, and Baby Steps   87
    Activity: A Success Ladder for Parents   94
  Behavioral Rehearsal   94
  Response Inhibition   96
  Fake It to Make It   99
  Pleasure Predicting   100
  Taking a Risk   102
  Prescribing Failure   103
  More Interventions for Perfectionism   104
    Sticking to the Plan   105
    Setting Realistic Expectations   106
    Planning Alternative Paths   107
  Increasing Motivation and Reducing Stress   109
    Reinforcement   109
    Reducing External Stressors   110
  Promoting Resilience   111
  Things to Remember   112
  Things to Do   113

Chapter 9. Patrick, Savannah, and Drew   **115**

Patrick   115

What Neighborhood Is Patrick In?   117

Helping Patrick Fight the Worry and OCD Monsters   117

Identifying Patrick's Irrational and Worrisome Thoughts   118

Changing Patrick's Thinking   118

Patrick's Success Ladder and Scare Steps   118

Response Inhibition   119

Strategies for Combating Worry   120

Coping Plan: Toolbox   120

Patrick's Success Ladder After Scaring Away
the Worry Monster   121

Patrick's Current Thinking   121

Savannah   122

What Neighborhood Is Savannah In?   123

Helping Savannah Fight the Worry Monster   123

Identifying Savannah's Worrisome Thinking   124

Challenging and Changing Savannah's Thinking   124

Reinforcing the Battle Plan   126

Drew   127

Identifying Drew's Worrisome Thinking   128

Changing Drew's Thinking   128

Setting Up a Behavior Plan   128

Drew's Toolbox   130

Chapter Summary   131

Things to Remember   132

Things to Do   132

Chapter 10. Making a Plan to Tame the Worry Monster   **133**

Making and Working the Plan   134

Step 1: Teach Your Child about the Brain   134

Step 2: Identify Body Feelings   135

Step 3: Externalize the Problem   135

Step 4: Make a Worry List   136

Step 5: Make a Success Ladder   137

Step 6: Identify Worrisome and Fearful Thinking   137

Step 7: Change and Modify Thinking   138

Step 8: Practice, Practice, Practice!   139

Step 9: Develop a Coping Toolbox   140

Working with Your Child's Teacher and School   141
And Poof, He's Gone!   142
Things to Remember   143
Things to Do   143

Chapter 11. Fine Tuning and Healthy Habits   **145**
Ideas for Fine Tuning the Plan   146
   Start with a Victory   146
   Look at Your Reinforcement Plan   146
   Try Working on a Different Worry or Fear   147
   Try a Different Thinking Strategy   147
   Distraction   147
   Add More Tools   148
Diet and Exercise   149
Sleep   150
What If the Worry Monster Still Won't Go Away?   151
Things to Remember   153
Things to Do   154

Chapter 12. Special Groups: Gifted, Twice-Exceptional (2e),
ADHD, and Other Learning and Processing Challenges   **155**
Gifted Children   155
   Common Characteristics of Gifted Children 156
   Overexcitabilities (OEs)   157
Attentional, Learning, and Processing Disorders   158
Twice-Exceptional (2e) Children   160
Special Kids and Special Accommodations   161
Things to Remember   163
Things to Do   164

Chapter 13. Do the Same Strategies Work for Adults?   **165**
Bringing It Home   168

Suggested Reading and Resources   **171**

Endnotes   **175**

References   **179**

Index   **183**

About the Author   **185**

Acknowledgments

The concepts in this book are not new; they are taken from the fields of neuroscience, cognitive behavioral therapy (CBT), narrative therapy, and mindfulness-based thinking. Each of those fields has contributed effective ideas and strategies for overcoming anxiety. I also am grateful for the work of many individuals who have influenced the way I work and think about conquering worry, anxiety, and fear. But here I will name a few to whom I am particularly indebted.

This book is especially influenced by a curriculum called Phobease™, developed by Dr. Howard Liebgold, a Kaiser Permanente physician from the California Bay Area. Affectionately known as Dr. FEAR (False Exaggerations Appearing Real), Dr. Liebgold taught Phobease classes for more than 25 years, helping more than 19,000 adults and children to successfully conquer their fears. I have worked with individuals who have taken his classes, and I have heard first-hand about the positive impact he has had on their lives. Dr. Liebgold significantly changed the lives of many and has inspired me to do the same. Sadly, Dr. Liebgold passed away just prior to the publication of this book. It is my hope that this book continues the important work that he began and to which he dedicated his life.

My work also has been influenced by a few significant training experiences I had while in graduate school. First, I attended two training seminars in cognitive behavioral therapy (CBT) by Jackie Persons, co-founder and Director of the Center for Cognitive Therapy in the San Francisco Bay Area. In these trainings, and in her book *Cognitive Therapy in Practice: A Case Formulation Approach*,[1] Dr. Persons taught me how to use CBT as a relationship-based approach that is interactive, collaborative, and based on a trusting relationship. I learned early on, and have experienced over and over again, that trust and acceptance is needed for healing and growth.

The other significant training experience I had that affected my approach to working with individuals with anxiety was my one-year externship in narrative therapy at the Mental Research Institute (MRI) in Palo Alto. The instructors, Jeff Zimmerman, Vickie Dickerson, and John Neal, taught me alternative ways of looking at people and the challenges and problems they face, including how people can "re-author" or "rewrite" the story of their lives.[2] This experience showed me that instead of focusing on what is "wrong" with people and what diagnosis they may have, people can be empowered to make changes using their strengths and focusing on what is "right" with them. This approach, which I found to be highly effective, is consistent with a newer movement in the field of psychology known as positive psychology.[3]

Dr. Liebgold's work and writings, Dr. Persons's caring and collaborative approach, and my mentors at MRI provided me with recipes for changing the story of people's lives, which I adapted further, adding a little of this and a little of that to make my own recipe for conquering and getting rid of the Worry Monster. It is this recipe that I will be sharing with you.

This book came out of a collaboration in Napa to break the silence on anxiety and other mental health issues and to get more children and teens support. Spearheading the grassroots-led community change work projects is the Director of Somos Napa/We Are Napa, Debbie Alter-Starr, MSW, LCSW. She first led a project to make a DVD titled *Taming the Worry Monster*, which was used by the Napa Valley Unified School District, Napa County Office of Education, and Napa Valley TV in both Spanish and English. Debbie also started programs to teach children and teens the techniques in this book, and she continues to advocate for more prevention programs. The goal is to encourage interested parents and teens to help change how communities address emotional health issues. Websites for ideas of how to do this are listed in the back of this book.

Many thanks to the collaborative partners: Napa Valley Unified School District, Napa County Office of Education, and Napa Valley TV. Special thanks to James Raymond, Executive Director of Napa Valley TV and Napa Valley Media, and his staff for their expertise and for transcribing the DVD, which became the foundation for this book. I am particularly indebted to Debbie for introducing me to Dr. Liebgold's work and for her continued creative ideas that have fueled my passion for helping people overcome anxiety and maximize their developmental potential, as well as contributing to fostering healthy communities.

I am grateful to the amazing group of people at Great Potential Press. First, to my publishers, Jim Webb and Jan Gore, for believing in the importance of this book and for their ideas, skill, and collaborative approach. They have put together an amazing team of individuals. I am grateful to all of them, and here I will highlight a few. I need to acknowledge Jen Ault, by far the most passionate editor in the world. Jen's commitment to this project was contagious, and it was a very meaningful collaboration. Thank you to Julee Hutchison for helping to bring the Worry Monster to life and for her patience and guidance in the process. Thank you to Katrina Durham for her ideas, support, and for helping to spread the word. And finally, thank you to Lisa Liddy for her diligence in laying out the book and for putting everything in just the right place.

I am grateful to my friends and colleagues who reviewed the original manuscript and offered wonderful suggestions: Debbie Alter-Starr, Joanna Haase, Dana Cope, and Laura Masters, and to my junior reviewer Jack Roy Cope. This book is made real by the authentic stories of special and courageous kids and their parents, whose stories are highlighted within its pages. You know who you are. You are an inspiration to me and now will be an inspiration to many who are trying to drive the Worry Monster away!

A special thank-you goes to my colleague Sally Baird for her support and collaboration in helping children and families take on and get rid of the Worry Monster. I would also like to thank three mentors, Anita Green, Allen Ewig, and Steve Hobbs. Thank you, Anita, for helping me become a writer by stretching me to "bring it home." I also want to thank you for *trying* to have me celebrate one milestone before moving on to the next one. Thank you, Allen, for helping me learn to grapple with the tough issues and understand that dealing with conflict is an important part of life. Thank you, Steve, for your guidance in life's continuing challenges and adventures.

Thank you to my friend and colleague Ed Amend for introducing me to Jim Webb and for supporting my career. A special thank-you goes to my friend and colleague Susan Daniels for her guidance, partnership, and support in helping me to realize that despite my lifelong aversion to writing, I am a creative person and an author who loves to write! I am also grateful for the dedicated friendship and support of Scott Tredennick, Rich Weingart, and my brother Mitch Peters.

Finally, this book would not be possible without the support and toleration of my family: to my kids, Sadie, Joe, and Tobie, for teaching me about the Worry Monster, how to help them (and how not to help them), and for their permission to tell their stories; also for embracing the concept of the Worry Monster, sharing their ideas for the book, and being interested (and pretending to be at times) in this project. Thank you to my parents, Mady and Richard, for their unwavering and unconditional love, interest, and support in my career and life. Last, but far from least, I thank my wife Lizzie, without whom all would not be possible. She is my partner in life, my business partner, my editor, and my friend who is committed to raising healthy kids and helping others do the same.

Introduction

Worry is like a rocking chair. It will give you something to do, but it won't get you anywhere.

~ Proverb

So How Did I Become an Anxiety Expert?

The topic of anxiety is very familiar to me, not just as a psychologist, but also personally. I didn't know what it was called when I was a child, but I knew that there was something heavy and unsettling that was often with me in my chest or stomach—something that made me feel a certain way, caused me to think certain thoughts, and made me do (or not do) certain things. I didn't like those feelings, but I thought they were normal.

Also as a young child, I remember how important it was to follow the "rules" and do the "right" things. I was super alert—very aware of my surroundings, what others were doing (and not doing), and what was "supposed" to happen. I remember being sent out of my second-grade classroom for talking. I was devastated and sat in the hallway crying. I felt like it was the end of the world. That was the only time I got in trouble in elementary school.

In school, I always hated to read and write. Writing was laborious, and I could never get my thoughts down on paper. I would sit staring at the blank page as my chest tightened and time ticked away. Reading also took a lot of energy. I would skim what I could, but mostly I tried to avoid the longer reading assignments. I felt nervous that my teacher would know that I wasn't doing the reading. I don't know how many excuses I had to come up with to tell my parents why I wasn't reading. Tests were nerve-wracking; I was always worried that I wouldn't have enough time to finish them, which was often true. Years later, I discovered that I was both dyslexic (difficulty reading) and dysgraphic (difficulty writing). I experienced first-hand the worry and anxiety that comes with having learning challenges and the fear of not doing well.

Even though I had so much difficulty with reading and writing, I also remember one of my cousins saying to me sarcastically, "So what's it like to always do everything right?" I wasn't sure what she meant. Was there any other way? I didn't realize at the time how hard I worked and how much effort it took to make sure I did everything "right." I was an expert at thinking about all the possibilities of what I should say and do in order to make sure that everything would be fine and that no one would feel hurt or upset with me.

My worries persisted beyond the early grades. Another story I sometimes share with my clients is a vivid memory I have of lying in bed at night while in seventh grade, going over my long list of things to worry about. When I got to the end of the list, I realized that I had checked everything off of it—I had worried about each thing on the list, and so I was done worrying. I felt a wonderful sense of calm—I didn't have anything left to worry about at that moment. But then, as quick as the feeling had come, it was gone, as my next thought was, "So what else do I need to worry about so that everything will be okay?" As you may already know, worrying (for an anxiety-prone individual) is a full-time job! And as a kid, I didn't know that there was any other way to think and feel.

In my teen years I played competitive tennis, and I know my coaches often wondered why I was not able to consistently perform in match play like I did in practice. They didn't realize (and neither did I) that I was so often worrying about losing that I wasn't able to focus on simply playing the game. I practiced a lot and had natural abilities, yet fear and worry (what I came to call the Worry Monster) often kept me from maximizing my potential. I played fearlessly in practice because in practice there was nothing to lose; fear of failure didn't apply there, but it sure did during tournaments. I thought, *What if I let my coach down? What will my parents think since they spent so much time, energy, and money supporting me?*

In high school, one of my closest friend's mother always talked about how good she felt about her son and me going out together at night because I was there as the "designated grown-up." After all, I used to think about all of the bad things that could happen and so therefore kept an eye on things.

Years later, in graduate school, I sat in my classes frustrated with my lack of knowledge. I read everything I could on every subject I studied, because we all know that in order to do well in a class, you need to know *everything* about the subject, right? Wrong! It wasn't until much later, when I learned that I was a perfectionist, that I realized I was comparing myself to my professors and supervisors who had been in the field 15 to 30 years. But yet I felt that I had to know what they knew, even though I was only in my early 20s and in graduate school.

As you can see, I was definitely a kid plagued by anxiety (although I worked hard to keep it under wraps). Worry, anxiety, and unhealthy perfectionism followed me into adulthood. And since apples don't usually fall far from the tree, I find that my kids get frequent visits from the Worry Monster, too. My three children have been afraid of things like being left at school, trying new activities, speaking or performing in front of others, answering the phone, making eye contact with new people, making a mistake, getting in trouble...and the list goes on. Do any of these sound familiar to you? Do you see these types of anxiety in your family? Fortunately, just as my kids have taught me about the Worry Monster, they also have helped me to understand how to help them change from worriers to warriors in order to tame this ogre and make him disappear.

Why This Book?

Eight percent of youth ages 13-18 have been given an anxiety diagnosis, with symptoms typically beginning at age six. Further, 18% of adults, or about 40 million people, are affected by anxiety in a given year.[4] These numbers only represent people who have sought help *and* have been diagnosed with anxiety. This means that there are even more people, far too many, living with anxiety than the numbers suggest. And those 40 million adults were once children who likely suffered from anxiety. But what if they had been given the tools to overcome their worry and fear as youngsters? Would that have had an impact on their future ability to manage and overcome their anxiety in adulthood? Yes, it would have. Learning coping strategies as a child clearly improves one's ability to cope as an adult.

Helping children learn about how worry and fear work in their brains and bodies, as well as how to manage these strong feelings, is helping to prepare them for dealing with life and its adversities. What I most love about this topic is that when we teach kids how the Worry Monster works, their lives change for the better. Sometimes the change is noticeable within days or weeks. Other times it takes a little longer to get kids fully on board with the idea of becoming a warrior in order to fight, tame, and defeat this monster. However, whether you see immediate results or more gradual ones, one thing is for sure: taming the Worry Monster is one of the most important personal growth experiences your child will ever have, and it will make his future brighter, more joyful, and more satisfying.

This book is the culmination of more than 20 years of working with children and families as a clinical psychologist, 13 years of raising my own children, and 43 years of living with my own tendencies to be a worrier and a perfectionist. It is a book that my friends, clients, and the parents with whom I have worked and who have come to hear me speak have been asking me to write because the principles and strategies I teach help their children *live* rather than *avoid* life.

I encourage all families to acquire the teaching tools I use, for the same reasons that most of us keep a hammer, screwdriver, garden clippers, and other all-purpose tools around the house.

In fact, this book could just as easily have been titled *A Parent's Toolbox for Raising Resilient Kids* because most children have fears and disappointments of some kind or other that these tools can be used with to foster greater resiliency and emotional intelligence—in other words, the ability to cope with life and manage one's emotions and behaviors.

It probably will not surprise you to learn that anxiety is on the rise in our society—with our children, in our communities, in our nation, and in the world at large. Most parents will likely admit that *we ourselves* are worrying more than we would like to. And it's not hard to find reasons for all of the fear and worrying going on. There's global warming, pending economic collapse, school shootings, war, budget deficits, our financial future, and of course, our children's education, happiness, and success. What's more, the news media seems even more focused these days on making us feel worried and scared—if that's possible.

While there are lots of things we can worry about, worrying does nothing but distract us from who we are and who we can be. Worry literally drains our energy and makes us afraid to take the risks we need to take to grow. It exhausts us as parents at a time when our children need us to guide them into developing a positive, worry-free outlook on life. Most importantly, worry and fear keep our children down, scared, miserable, and unnecessarily insecure with themselves and their ability to not only survive, but to thrive.

The good news is that you can help change this. Through my own experiences with worry and anxiety, watching what it does to my children, and seeing how it affects the children and families I have worked with over the years, I have become committed to the vision of a worry-free world. I am not suggesting that we ignore the realities of the world, but I am advocating that we actively choose not to let those realities result in a life filled with worry and fear. I have both experienced and witnessed the debilitating effects of worry, anxiety, and fear. They can be crippling and can result in a life not fully lived. Too many people live with constant doubt, self-criticism, and pain. Too many people live with talents they never pursued or developed or with dreams and goals they never risked. It doesn't have to be that way.

About This Book

This book is a "How To" recipe book designed to help you help your child overcome worry and fear by teaching you a number of easy-to-follow strategies that you can then teach your child. The book takes an approachable and non-stigmatizing view of ways you can teach your child about "how we tick" as human beings and then helps her learn how to master parts of her body and mind so that she will be better equipped to deal with life as it comes and live to her fullest potential.

This book is about teaming up with your child to help her do the most courageous thing she will ever have to do: become a warrior in order to fight and tame the Worry Monster. I have written with language that you can use to talk to your child about worry, anxiety, and fear and how she can become a warrior instead of a worrier by conquering these feelings. It is the same language that I use in my office daily to help children and their parents learn about the Worry Monster and how to drive him away. Also, it is the same language I use with my own children.

You and your child will learn about how our bodies are programmed to keep us alive and how we sometimes go into "survival mode" even when we don't need it. You will learn about how the body feels during the "fight or flight" response and which "whoosh" feelings your child experiences. You will learn about who the Worry Monster is and how he uses thoughts to make your child (and you) feel worried and scared. You will then learn how to help your child change her worried thinking and practice specific behaviors to make the Worry Monster go away. You will find out how to help your child create a "toolbox" that she can carry with her wherever she goes so that she is ready to fight the Worry Monster when he tries to mess with her. Finally, you will become aware that the information and strategies that work for your child will also work just as effectively for you.

How do I know this recipe works? Children who initially came into my office who were afraid of failing, swimming, petting dogs, sleeping in their own bed, going to school, taking tests, trying new things, and having sleepovers returned to my office over the years with smiles on their faces and told me about their repeated victories over the Worry Monster. Meanwhile their parents sat with equally big smiles on their faces watching their children share their success stories. Parents described to me how their family life had improved because their child was now able to go to the park, attend a party, or just laugh and relax more.

As you read this book, talk to your child about what you are reading. Explain the interesting and helpful strategies you are learning and how you are using them yourself. Express excitement and confidence when telling your child that there is a way to fight the Worry Monster in order to free her from her worries and fears. Our tone of voice, as much as the words we use, help our children feel hopeful. Let your child know that her worry and fear are temporary, and with courage, she will learn ways to manage her worry and feel better. You will be serving as a positive, confident role model, showing your child how you are facing your own fears with the same tools.

Finally, please know that this book is not intended to be a replacement for counseling or therapy. However, the strategies I teach within these pages can be used in conjunction with therapy. In fact, I encourage parents to share what they are learning with their child's counselor or therapist so that everyone involved in supporting the child has as many tools as possible at their disposal to help the child overcome worry and fear.

Okay, it's time to fight the Worry Monster and make your worrier a warrior. Ready? Let's do this!

Note: If you would like to have a picture of the Worry Monster to refer to as you read this book or to give to your child, a full-color image of him is available at http://bit.ly/ParentWarrior or http://bit.ly/ TheWorryMonster. You can go to either of those websites to find a pdf file, which you can print and use any time you feel that having your child actually see the monster will help the two of you do battle against him and conquer him.

CHAPTER 1

Who Is the Worry Monster?

Worry is a useless mulling over of things we cannot change.
~ Peace Pilgrim

Some Examples of Worriers

Before we learn about who the Worry Monster is, I want to tell you about a few young people I know and the different challenges they face every day.

Sierra is six years old and in first grade. She is afraid to be alone, so she follows her mother around the house and needs her to come with her into to her bedroom, and even into the bathroom. She calls to her mother when she wakes up—at all hours of the night—to come be with her. Drop-off at school is difficult because Sierra clings to her mother and says she doesn't want her to go. Sierra's mom has to stay with her at birthday parties and after-school activities or else Sierra will refuse to participate in them.

Ben is nine years old and a fourth grader. He worries about bad things happening, though he is not sure exactly what the bad things are. He is always asking his mother and his teacher for reassurance that things will be okay—

for example, that he is doing his schoolwork the way he is supposed to. Ben worries that he will get in trouble at school, and that his classmates may, too. He bites his fingernails and chews on his shirt but isn't aware he is doing so. He often complains of having a stomachache.

Tanner is 10, and he needs to be in charge of everything. Others see him as controlling and bossy but are initially drawn to him because of his energy and great ideas. Tanner has trouble keeping friends because he doesn't listen to anyone else's ideas and makes up rules to favor himself in the games he plays with others. When things don't go his way, or he loses, or kids refuse to play with him, he lashes out at them verbally and erupts emotionally. He always comes up with some reason why the other children deserved what happened or why it is their fault.

Phil is 10 and in fifth grade. He always seems to be worrying about something that could happen. He works hard to do well in school and wants to please his parents and teachers. Most people don't know how much he worries because he keeps it to himself. He frequently believes that he will stop worrying once he completes a project or after playing well in an important soccer game, but there always seems to be something new to worry about.

Jenny is 11 years old and in the sixth grade. She has started at a new middle school, and her best friends are all attending a different school. Jenny says that she feels nauseous at school and fears that she may get sick and throw up. Her teachers say she seems to be in a daze during class. Jenny often begs to stay home from school because she feels sick. When she does stay home, she seems fine. She also seems to be normal or "herself" on weekends.

Casey is 12, and she feels like she has to touch things a certain way to feel okay. If she touches one of her legs, she feels like she has to touch the other leg in the same way so that they are balanced. When she walks into her room, she has to touch her door five times or else she feels funny. She counts numbers in her head while she's walking to school, and if she loses track of the numbers, she has to go back to the last place she remembered them and start again. She says that if she doesn't do these things, something bad might happen.

Mateo is 15 years old, in the ninth grade, and has always struggled with social situations. He has trouble looking people in the eyes when he talks to them, and he fears that he will have nothing interesting to say or will say something stupid and be laughed at. Mateo feels like everyone else does things better than he does and that he will never achieve his goals in life. When things don't go as he plans, he becomes very upset and overwhelmed and says things like, "What if I can't take care of myself when I grow up?" and "What if I never have a meaningful friendship?" His parents say he seems to carry the weight of the world on his shoulders. He stays home after school and on weekends playing video games and cannot be encouraged to call kids he knows from school to make plans with them. He doesn't want to join activities at his school because he's sure he will be no good at them and that his classmates won't like him.

Sophie, age 17 and a junior in high school, has always been a high achiever, mostly receiving A's and A+'s in school. She also plays several sports and volunteers in the community. She is so busy and takes such hard classes that she stays up late studying because feels that she needs to do her work perfectly. Even though her work is excellent, she is rarely proud of her accomplishments. She experiences life as "a grind." She is often tense and stressed, and she worries about what will happen if she doesn't get into a top college.

Do any of these examples sound like children you know? Does your child exhibit some of these feelings or behaviors? These are common worries and fears for children. Some children worry about their safety and that of their loved ones, others worry about making mistakes, some worry about being laughed at, and others worry about not living up to their own and others' standards. And some kids just seem to worry about everything!

At first we thought it was just our own kids who had anxiety—anxiety passed down through both me and their father's extended family members, so I felt bad about that. When I took a risk, though, and started talking about these issues with others, I found out how many of my friends and my children's friends were living with anxiety too! I'm so glad I started learning about anxiety and talking about it.
                                              ~ mother of two warriors

What if It Seems Your Child Doesn't Want to Be Helped?

Even though your child may be used to worrying and being scared, and he may say he doesn't want to do anything to face his worries and fears, *trust me,* he does *not* want to feel like this. He just doesn't know another way to think and feel about certain situations, and he may be scared of change. I can absolutely assure you, however, that he *does* want to feel different. He *does not* want to live with worry and live in fear. He *does not* like having stomachaches, headaches, and a tight chest. Even if he can't admit it out loud yet, he wants you to help him feel better and make all of his negative feelings go away. So that is what you are going to do. You are going to teach him about the Worry Monster—how the Worry Monster works, what he does to trick us into feeling bad, and how to make him go away.

Our kids were initially resistant to us trying to help them cope better. They came around when they realized that we were not giving up on this topic of facing our fears and that we could actually help them feel better. I think they were also relieved that we took charge of this situation as their parents.

~ father of two warriors

Creating Separation

The Worry Monster is a very useful concept for helping kids wrap their mind around something that often feels like it controls them, something that is a part of them that permeates their being—a part of their "real self." The idea of using a concept like the Worry Monster to talk about anxiety comes from an approach that helps people "re-author" or "rewrite" their life. A key component of this approach is to *externalize* the problem so it becomes something outside of them—not their real self after all. Separating the problem from the person by labeling it and giving it a name externalizes it and allows the person to feel that he may be able to control it. Thus, the experience of worry, anxiety, and/or fear is given the name of "Worry Monster," and some space or separation is developed between the experience and the child. Because of this, the problem can be told to "get out of town." I have found this approach to be very helpful, as it gives the child perspective and room to consider his intense feelings and behaviors as something other than just a part of who he is.

If your child wants to call anxiety by some name other than "Worry Monster," that's fine too, so long as he makes his anxiety something that is *not* him, *not* his friend, and *not* something that protects him, either. A teen, for example, may think "Worry Monster" sounds too childish and instead could use a narrative of something else—maybe having the meanest bully in the world living inside of his head, and he needs to tell that lying, no good *@$&% bully to get lost. Since worried teens start out as worried children, however, some teens might like the idea of the Worry Monster, so give this concept a try even with adolescents. Other common monsters that children and teens might want to refer to are the OCD Monster and the Perfectionist Monster. As you will learn, these monsters are all members of the same gang and are related to each other. They are like a bunch of hooligans that gang up on your child to make his life miserable. Your child will need to become a warrior if he is going to stand up to them, control them, and banish them!

Pulling Back the Curtain

The idea of a Worry Monster is a key concept that allows you and your child to work together to battle this bully and push him out of your home and your life. The primary reason this approach works is that the more we understand anxiety, the more we can demystify it, overpower it, overcome it, and make it go away. The concept is quite simple, but the act of making worry go away takes a lot of persistence and courage. Your child or teen is truly being heroic to face her fears. If you have anxiety yourself, you probably understand this. As one courageous child I know said, "The Worry Monster goes away and comes back. Sometimes it's harder than other times to make it go away."

Let's take a look at a famous example of what we are talking about. Most of us have seen *The Wizard of Oz* (and some of us may still have nightmares about the wicked witch and her flying monkeys). Remember the scene in which Dorothy, Tin Man, Scarecrow, and the Cowardly Lion are in front of the big, scary Wizard, who's making terrifying noises with smoke billowing all around him? The Wizard seems cruel and callous, and they are petrified and shaking. Then it happens; the smallest character tugs at the curtain covering the most powerful being. Toto pulls the drape back, and they all find out that the Wizard is a small, middle-aged man on a power trip working levers and manipulating reality. Dorothy, in surprise and anger, says, "I think you are a very bad man!" to which the Wizard replies, "I'm really a very good man, but I'm a very bad wizard!"

The monsters that we think are so great and all-powerful often turn out to be illusions, and we can fight and tame them if we have the courage to do so. When we think back to Dorothy and her friends, what do we see? All of a sudden they're strong, courageous, and smart! They start problem solving, and before we know it, Dorothy is on her way back home to comfort and happiness.

So there you have it. The Wizard of Oz is a metaphor for the Worry Monster and how we are going to fight him. The Worry Monster is a big bully who we think has a ton of power because he tricks us into thinking he is powerful. In fact, we all have in ourselves the strength to cope, persevere, and figure things out. As a wise boy I know who knows the Worry Monster well told me: "We are all stronger than we think."

In the chapters to come, you are going to read some information first and then start talking to your child about who the Worry Monster is, what he tells your child to make her worried and scared, and also what thinking and behavior strategies your child can use to make the Worry Monster smaller and less significant in her life, until finally—poof—he disappears. The Worry Monster will become a regular part of your vocabulary, as you and your child talk about him and team up against him to lessen his power. You can also show your child a picture of the Worry Monster to show her what a ridiculous goofball this monster really is. (You can download a full-color image of the Worry Monster by visiting http://bit.ly/ParentWarrior or http://bit.ly/TheWorryMonster.) Why do we let this creature bully us? Time to start laughing at the Worry Monster *with* your child. Taunt him, tease him, and belittle him. Worry Monster, your days are numbered!

It is important to remember, however, that your child, and especially your teen, may feel a sense of shame and guilt about her worries and fears. It is important to have these conversations in a neutral and nonjudgmental tone so that she can get beyond her shame and guilt and start to take the Worry Monster on. It may be helpful for you to think back to when you were a child and may have worried, felt scared, or felt guilty for thinking a certain way. This will help you "walk in your child's shoes" and maybe have some compassion for yourself as well (your current self or your child version).

Things to Remember

- ✔ Children do not like feeling worried and scared.
- ✔ The Worry Monster is a bully.
- ✔ The worry and fear (the Worry Monster) is not part of them.
- ✔ You are going to help your child drive the Worry Monster away.

Things to Do

- ✔ Tell your child about the Worry Monster—that he is a mythical creature who tries to make us feel worried and scared.

- ✔ Offer hope that you and your child will be able to do things that make the Worry Monster go away.

- ✔ Show your child a picture of the goofy Worry Monster, or ask your child to make a drawing of the Worry Monster— what she thinks he looks like.

CHAPTER 2

Anxiety and the Fear Response

Our fatigue is often caused not by work, but by worry, frustration, and resentment.

~ Dale Carnegie

Now that you have an understanding of who the Worry Monster is and you know that we are going to use this concept to help your child take action to defeat his fears and worries, it is important to understand what worry or anxiety is and how it works. There are many different definitions of anxiety, but we are going to use a simple one that makes sense in order to meet our goal of taking the Worry Monster down and driving him out of town.

Simply put, anxiety is an irrational fear:[5] "They're all going to laugh at me." "Something bad is going to happen." "I'll get lost." "What if you don't come back for me?" "What if I make a mistake?" These fears feel very real to our children, both in their bodies and in their minds. And yet they are irrational thoughts given to them by the Worry Monster.

You and your child are going to learn that the Worry Monster tricks us into feeling our uncomfortable and scary feelings by messing with our thoughts. What will be most confusing to your child is that there often is a slight grain of truth to the fear behind the fearful thinking, which "proves" to your child that his fearful thinking is realistic or "the truth." The Worry Monster's main strategy is to convince us that the very, very, very small chance that something bad might happen is what's actually going to happen, and when it does happen, the results will be beyond our ability to cope.

How many times have you tried to reason with your child when he was afraid but he still said, "Well, something *could* happen to you," or "They *might* make fun of me," or "We *could* get in a car accident"? Yes, these are all possibilities, but the Worry Monster tricks your child into thinking that the possibilities are guaranteed to happen and that when they do happen, they will ruin his life. But the Worry Monster is fundamentally a bully. He bullies us into thinking certain things, feeling certain things, and then behaving in certain ways, which are counterproductive for our lives.

The Survival Response

Now that we have a simple definition of anxiety—an irrational fear—we need to talk about an important part of our human, biological makeup: the fear response. Fear actually is good because, in short, it keeps us alive. Think back (even though we do not have a personal memory of this) to when we humans were cave people and hunters and gathers. We lived among other tribes who wanted our stuff, as well as big animals who wanted to eat us. We needed (and continue to need) fear to mobilize us for survival purposes.[6] That's why we have a "fight or flight" response.

Here is how the fear response works. In our brains, there is a very small almond-shaped group of neurons, called the amygdala, that resides in our limbic system, which is the emotional center of our bodies. The amygdala is the fear center of the brain. Its primary job is to sense danger and therefore to keep us alive. Imagine having a danger sensor in your head that is always on alert and always surveying for danger. That's what our amygdala does.

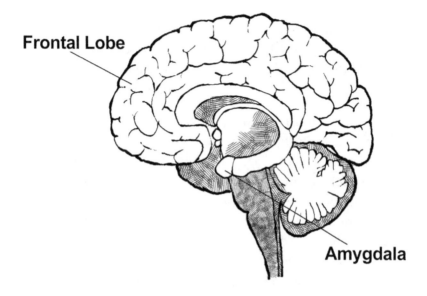

Frontal Lobe

Amygdala

Here's the catch, however: when we feel fear or anxiety, we are usually *not* in a life-threatening situation, yet our amygdala is going off and the alarm bells are ringing. Let me say this very important point another way. When it comes to the Worry Monster, our amygdala is turned on and activated for action even though we don't need it to be activated. It's like having a car alarm that is too sensitive and goes off all the time over nothing. If you are walking down a dark alley and see shadows and there's no one around and you didn't bring your cell phone, that's a good time for your amygdala's alarm bells to go off. It is not productive, however, to have that same feeling when walking through the lunchroom at school with your friends. But it *feels* the same. Fortunately, most of the time we're not in dark alleys in the middle of the night.

Amygdala is our family's new favorite word. We all realize that it gets activated in different situations for each of us, which has been a cool discovery. We all have fears and anxiety but about different things, and now we know what is happening in our brains and not to let it control our decision to move forward. We say to each other, "My amygdala is kicking in," when something is freaking us out, and just realizing that makes it better. Our favorite quote from our son after I first told him about it was, "I must have a really big amygdala!" We laughed really hard at that one.

~ mother of a warrior

When the amygdala senses danger, it sends messages to our adrenal glands to start producing as much adrenaline as possible in order to help us either fight or take flight—in short, to escape quickly! It's actually quite simple, and we certainly should appreciate how our body is designed to keep us alive. When the adrenal gland gets the signal from our amygdala to pump as much adrenaline as possible, boy does it go to town, sometimes like firemen swinging a fire hose! Surges of adrenalin running through our body increase our heart rate and breathing rate and divert blood from our stomach and brain into our muscles to make us stronger. We are instantly turned into running and fighting machines with one purpose: survival!

So that you know just how powerful the physiological response of adrenaline is and what symptoms it can produce, here is a list of symptoms (in alphabetical order) caused by excessive adrenaline:[7]

Blurred or distorted vision, chest pain, choking sensations, clenched teeth, cold hands and feet, depersonalization, detachment, diarrhea, disassociation (depersonalization, detachment, and disassociation are what make children and adults fear they are going crazy), *dizziness, dry mouth, easily startled and hyper-vigilant, faintness, fatigue, fidgetiness, headache, holding one's breath, hot or cold flashes, hyperventilation, jumpiness, light-headedness, loss of appetite, loss of balance, lump in the throat, muscle aches, muscle tension, muscle weakness, nausea, numbness, palpitations, rapid heart rate, restlessness, shakiness, shallow breathing, shortness of breath, skin problems (itching and burning), smothering sensation, stomach pain, sweating, tight chest, tingling sensation, trembling, trouble swallowing, tunnel vision, unsteady feeling (knees shake), urinary frequency, urinary and bowel urgency, vomiting, weakness.*

Can you believe it? All of these symptoms can be explained by excessive adrenalin! I can remember two particular experiences in college when I was clearly experiencing too much adrenaline. The first is when I went bungee jumping with friends off a high bridge, and the second was as a student painter on a ladder three stories high. In both situations, my legs started shaking uncontrollably, like I was in a cartoon. My chest tightened, and I became dizzy and light-headed. That did not help me in either of those situations!

I have found it incredibly helpful to explain the fight or flight response to children so they better understand their bodily sensations and so they become aware of the purpose of these adrenalin surges when our amygdala alarm bell goes off. Knowing about this is one of the key components in helping children understand how the Worry Monster makes them feel, as well as helping to demystify what the scary feelings are. This allows them to identify when the Worry Monster is visiting and doing his sneaky work to make our lives miserable.

As Dr. Liebgold explains in detail, here is why our body feels the way it does when we are scared:[8]

✔ *Heart and Lungs*: Your heart beats faster; your chest gets tight; you breathe faster and feel like you can't get enough air. This occurs so that you can fight and run better. Your body speeds up your heart and lungs in order to send more blood into your muscles so they are stronger.

✔ *Stomach*: You experience stomach pain, nausea, and maybe even diarrhea. This happens because much of the blood leaves your stomach and intestines and pumps into your heart, lungs, and muscles in case it is needed to make you a fighting and running machine. Your amygdala is more concerned with your ability to escape saber-tooth tigers than with whether you digest your macaroni and cheese.

✔ *Brain*: You feel dizzy, light-headed, and have strange feelings, like you're about to faint, you're going crazy, or you're losing control. The reason is that your blood has to leave your brain to get into your heart, lungs, and muscles.

✔ *Arms and Legs*: You start sweating and get cold hands, numbness, shaking, trembling, muscle tenseness, and even pain. The reason this happens is that your blood leaves your skin so that you won't bleed as much if you get hurt. Isn't that cool? We are so designed for survival that the blood even leaves our skin so we can do better in battle!

So as you can see, our entire body is focused on keeping us alive by diverting blood into our arms and legs so we can fight and run. Blood leaves our stomach because we don't need to digest our macaroni and cheese when we are running for our life. It should make a little more sense now why children may have stomach cramps, have an upset stomach, or have to go to the bathroom over and over again when they experience anxiety.

Next, blood leaves our brain because we don't need to solve complex problems when we are running for our lives. "No distractions! Run fast! Push hard! Harder! Faster!" But what happens? We start to feel dizzy; we start to get headaches; we start to feel like we're going nuts. Our minds are swirling because all of the blood is leaving our brains so we can run and fight—it's that simple!

Kids find all of this information fascinating; they especially love the part about how the blood goes away from the surface of our arms and legs. That's why we get tingling sensations in those parts of our bodies. That way we can be wounded in battle and not bleed to death. Isn't that fascinating? So we can explain to them: "Tingling? Oh, the blood is leaving your arms. Is there anyone going to attack us? No? Then we can let the blood go back into your arms. You're going to be okay." We are trying to get them to understand the physical feelings they are experiencing and to emotionally distance themselves from these sensations—to be outside "scientific observers" of a fascinating (and frequently annoying) biological phenomena.

It is crucial to help your child let go of her emotional connection to her physical experiences. For example, some kids may think that they should avoid school in order to avoid having stomachaches. We want them to solve the stomachache problem a different way—by turning off their body's overactive emergency response system.

As we'll discuss later, every child has his or her own physiological reaction to anxiety. Some kids' heads get hot. Some kids have shortness of breath. Other kids start to sweat. A 10-year-old client of mine recently described her feeling as the "whoosh" feeling because she felt like she was on a roller coaster (one she didn't want to be on!).

You can teach your child about her own unique response to the Worry Monster. How can we know when the Worry Monster's in town? How do we know when the Worry Monster is in your home? What are your child's "whoosh" feelings?

An important thing to remember is that the scary "whoosh" feelings *always* go away. They often feel like they won't, but they will, just like an itch. Another strategy for getting through these intense and uncomfortable feelings is to "ride the wave."[9] This refers to merely hanging on for the ride, knowing that it won't last long and will be over soon.

The Worry Monster is "turning on" your child's emotional brain and "turning off" her great thinking brain. He doesn't like us to talk about him and challenge him, but we are going to be talking about using our thinking brain to outsmart the Worry Monster. We'll be developing a language and a greater sense of awareness to help your child identify when the Worry Monster is visiting her so that we can take steps to chase him out of town!

Things to Remember

- ✔ Our bodies are built to survive.

- ✔ Our amygdala's job is to sense danger and trigger our survival or "fight or flight" response.

- ✔ Excessive adrenaline is deployed to make us into super-human fighting or running machines.

- ✔ This adrenaline makes our body—brain, stomach, heart, lungs, arms, and legs—feel a certain way.

- ✔ We need to help our kids turn on their thinking brain in order to turn down their emotional brain.

- ✔ The more we talk about the Worry Monster, the weaker he gets.

Things to Do

- ✔ Teach your child about the survival or "fight or flight" response.

- ✔ Explain to your child the brain's amygdala and the role of adrenaline.

- ✔ Teach your child about how too much adrenaline affects the brain, heart, lungs, stomach, arms, and legs.

- ✔ Tell your child about "whoosh" feelings, and ask her where she gets her "whooshes."

- ✔ Let your child know that she is going to learn about how she will use her big thinking brain to overpower her small emotional brain.

CHAPTER 3

Types of Anxiety and What They Look Like

Worry does not empty tomorrow of its sorrow. It empties today of its strength.

~ Corrie Ten Boom

It helps to know some of the different types of anxiety to get a sense of what general area or "neighborhood" your child's pattern of anxiety most fits into. We are not concerned, by referring to these "neighborhoods," with making an actual diagnosis; rather, we are trying to outsmart the Worry Monster by knowing more about where he hangs out and some different ways in which he operates. Of course, some neighborhoods are scarier than others, but a warrior can learn how to handle himself in tough neighborhoods or can manage to stay away from some neighborhoods altogether. Please don't let the names and descriptions of the types of anxieties listed in this chapter alarm you. They may be scary words, but the types of Worry Monsters are actually rather common to many people who have learned to tame them.

Generalized Anxiety

Generalized anxiety is basically the general and widespread Worry Monster. It describes what happens when a child or adult experiences ongoing worry that is excessive, pervasive, and constant about most topics ("When will you be home?" "What if something bad happens?" "Do I look okay?" "What if I make a mistake?" "What if I don't get picked?"). We're all worried about our kids, and sometimes we get a little out of hand with that worry, and then they start worrying about themselves, too. Worry truly can be contagious! This is just a gentle reminder that we need to manage our own Worry Monster at the same time we are helping our child manage his.

Panic Attacks

A panic attack is a surge of fear that is comprised of normal body responses yet occurs when those responses are not needed.[10] It is an onslaught of physiological sensations caused by adrenalin flooding the body, which leads an individual to incorrectly believe that she might be having a heart attack, pass out, or literally die. The heart beats faster and faster, and the person fears that her heart may never stop the rapid beating. In addition, the person breathes very rapidly but in such a shallow way that she can't take in enough oxygen, and there is a build-up of carbon dioxide in the blood that triggers a feeling of panic.[11] Panic attacks are the purest form of the fear response, and they are responsible for an enormous number of visits to the emergency room by both adults and children.

There is also a less intense version of the panic attack that children often experience, which I refer to as an "anxiety attack," and it can range from mild to moderate to severe. Though less intense, it still feels awful! A lot of children have these lower-grade versions of panic attacks when they're in anxiety-provoking situations.

> *Whenever my daughter Adrienne takes a math test, she feels dizzy; she says she can't remember what she learned and knows how to do, and she starts to think she's going to fail the test. Once she starts thinking this, she starts to*

sweat. Next she has trouble breathing. She tells us that she just wants to run out of the classroom, but we've encouraged her to tell her teacher that she feels sick so that she's allowed to go to the nurse's office instead. Her teacher is supportive and has informed us that Adrienne looks pale when this happens.

~ mother of a warrior

When I have a panic/anxiety attack, I start hyperventilating and thinking that there are going to be a whole bunch of natural disasters like tsunamis, earthquakes, fires, hurricanes, tornados, et cetera, or that there is going to be a murder or something—anything. Everything bad is going to happen.

~ 15-year-old warrior

Agoraphobia

Agoraphobia is the term we use when a person thinks he is about to have a panic attack, and he fears that he will be unable to escape the situation once he starts to panic. It is somewhat like a fear of becoming fearful. Because the individual wants to avoid the panic attack, as well as related feelings of embarrassment, he avoids places and situations where he worries that he might experience an attack. Whenever he runs away or avoids a situation, his anxiety is reduced. Whew! Except that now his running away and avoiding has been reinforced, making it even more difficult for him to overcome his fear. Because of this, avoidance behaviors can be very challenging to overcome.

Over time, agoraphobia can restrict your child from going out to enjoy many different kinds of activities. Let's say, for example, that your child has a panic attack one day in a large supermarket and then becomes afraid it's going to happen again. As a result, he refuses to go to all supermarkets or any store resembling a supermarket. Next, he gets the same bodily sensations and fears when your family is in a restaurant, which has similar food smells, so he decides he is not going to any more restaurants. He then comes to fear a variety of other buildings. Before long you are approaching a full-blown agoraphobia situation, like you see on TV sometimes, in which a person doesn't leave his or her house for years.

This is a perfect example of why it is so important to help our children face their fears when they first arise so that they don't grow. Agoraphobia is the most extreme example of fears that can mushroom if not dealt with when they first appear.

It is also important to note that kids who focus strongly on controlling their environment and their life may have a subtle form of this type of anxiety. Often, no one realizes that the child is afraid to go outside or to new activities or situations because he is afraid of having an anxiety attack. Kids can be very good at rationalizing all of the reasons they don't want to do this or that in their attempts to keep the Worry Monster at bay. A little investigating may be warranted to get to the bottom of their avoidance behaviors.

Obsessive-Compulsive Disorder (OCD)

OCD is characterized by an anxiety-producing, often persistent thought or idea—an obsession—that is both intrusive and embarrassing. A compulsion is a repetitive, intentional behavior that is done to try to relieve the anxiety produced by the thought. Most people think of OCD in terms of flipping light switches on and off repeatedly or washing one's hands excessively. These are common OCD behaviors. However, behind these behaviors are repetitive irrational thoughts that are very distressing and that won't go away. In most cases, the child with OCD has to do some specific thing to feel okay, like touch the doorway in a certain place when walking through it, or tapping each leg the same number of times, or kissing you on both sides of your face before bedtime.

> *Our son Walt is an exceptional student, athlete, and kind young man. He worries about his school performance and has to do certain things to make sure he doesn't fail or become "bad." These behaviors consist of touching everything an even*

number of times with both hands, repeating the last words of sentences in his head, and making sure he doesn't step over a line without repeating what he was thinking as he steps over the line. He also often has to erase words that he writes if he writes them while worrying about turning into a bad student, and he has to repeat certain things in his head a certain number of times so he feels okay.

~ mother of a warrior

While there is almost always a distressing thought connected to compulsive behaviors, sometimes it can be a challenge to figure out what that distressing thought actually is. Also, children can have compulsions without identifiable obsessions. We must remember that many children have magical thinking and even OCD-like quirks or characteristics, and these tendencies are frequently found in children who are cognitively advanced and considered gifted. In those instances, the behaviors, though seemingly irrational, are not necessarily indicators of OCD.

Specific Phobia

Sometimes anxiety is tightly focused. A specific phobia is a restrictive fear that is excessive, unreasonable, and is triggered by the presence or anticipation of a specific object like a snake or spider or a frightening situation such as public speaking or flying in an airplane. These phobias are usually easy to avoid, such as avoiding insects by never going camping and avoiding planes by never flying, though there are some exceptions. For example, a fear of dogs can cause significant difficulty for a child because it is difficult to always avoid them.

My daughter's phobias have been extremely varied. She had a phobia of the number 3 when she was a preschooler—we didn't realize at the time it was a phobia, though. Later she had phobias of bugs, then snails. During the rainy season—and this was when she was eight years old—we had to pick her up and carry her from the car into buildings due to her fear of snails. Later she developed a phobia of her school principal, and it was hard to get her back to school in the fall.

~ father of a warrior

Social Phobia

A social phobia is a persistent fear of social or performance situations in which a child is exposed to unfamiliar people or to possible scrutiny from others. This is basically the fear of embarrassment or humiliation. "The kids are going to laugh at me." "They're making fun of me." "Look how they're looking at me." "I don't belong here." "What are they going to say?" "What if I look funny?" Now, there could be some truth to these statements, right? We all know kids who actually have these experiences, but what we're talking about when we refer to social anxiety is when the response is extreme and significantly affecting or interfering with a child's life, whether or not she has had some of these experiences at one time or another. Examples of extreme behavior include refusal to go to school or to participate in school activities and refusal to attend social events.

I worry about not being very good at something and then being embarrassed and having people laugh at me and make fun of me. I also worry about not being able to find where it is I am supposed to go or ending up in the wrong place and/ or being told that I am in the wrong place in front of people (for example, going into the wrong classroom and sitting down and the teacher calls you out in front of everyone).

~ 15-year-old warrior

Post-Traumatic Stress Disorder (PTSD)

PTSD is term familiar to many people, as so many of our veterans experience it once they come home from war. They have lived through various traumas, and they have nightmares or flashbacks to the incidents. This same term also applies to anyone, including a child, who experiences some kind of frightening trauma and cannot seem to recover from it. Usually is it a situation in which there is intense fear of permanent injury or damage. Sometimes it can be a near-death experience or watching someone else's near-death experience. A child watching parents physically fight may fear the death of a parent. A child who has been abused or who experiences harsh physical punishment may have PTSD. A child with PTSD may experience emotional numbing, nightmares, and flashbacks of the traumatic experience. The child will avoid situations that remind him of the traumatic situation, and he may be jumpy and nervous and/or have extreme emotional meltdowns.

There are lots of kids who have gone through traumatizing situations in their home environments, in the community, or at school. It doesn't matter whether a child experiences or witnesses violence or significant parental conflict, is bullied by peers, or is chronically misunderstood by teachers for being different and quirky; many children have *some* of the symptoms of PTSD, which I refer to as having "PTSD with a small *p*." These kids are often afraid and avoidant of situations that were (or are) traumatic for them, with the result that they can be moody, irritable, and depressed.

Separation Anxiety

Separation anxiety is when a child is afraid to leave her parents and feels that something bad is going to happen to her or her parents while they are apart. When your child is quite young, it is developmentally appropriate for her to not want to be away from you. She may cry every day before school or when you leave her at preschool (or both)—at least until you are out of sight, and then the teacher reports later that she was fine. Your child may need you to stay with her during dance class, soccer practice, and parties. This may go on for a while, and it could just be a developmental stage that almost always goes away. However, if your child continues to need your presence by about the time she enters kindergarten, she is likely experiencing some anxiety that qualifies as a Worry Monster.

Cody gets anxious at bedtime. My husband and I work late, and we have a babysitter for him—an older woman he really likes. But even with her there, Cody forces himself to stay awake until his father and I both get home and get to bed, even if it is really late, because he worries that something bad will happen to us; he can only relax once we have returned safely.

~ mother of a warrior

Remember that it is not uncommon for bright and sensitive kids to feel more insecure when their parents are not around and to need them for a few years longer than most other kids do. Highly gifted children tend to need their parents to help them interpret the world and to feel safe due to their sensitivities for much longer than what is typical for average-ability children. (This is further elaborated in Chapter 12.)

Perfectionism

Perfectionism is another way in which the Worry Monster (or his close friend, the Perfectionism Monster) plays havoc with our lives. It is not an actual anxiety diagnosis, but it nonetheless can be pervasive and debilitating for our children. The core feature of perfectionism is a fear of failure.[12] You should probably know that there is some disagreement in the field about perfectionism. Some experts on the subject think that there is a good kind of perfectionism and a bad kind of perfectionism, or positive perfectionism and negative perfectionism.[13] Positive perfectionism is a character trait that helps us do our best work and try to always be at our best. Negative perfectionism is when perfectionism goes too far so that we feel we can never be good enough. However, some experts believe that perfectionism is always bad and ultimately results in our never feeling good enough and never feeling as though we measure up.[14] Either way, we are talking here about a kind of thinking that is typically negative, self-critical, defeating, and that leads to avoidance. A perfectionistic child would rather not try a new task, for example, than risk not doing it well or failing.

Our goal is to help perfectionists strive for excellence rather than perfection because striving for excellence involves failure and risk taking.[15] Perfectionism in the form of having to be perfect keeps our children from trying anything that takes effort and at which they could struggle, stumble, and fail. In short, it prevents them from showing what they can do and putting their best foot forward.

I frequently work with perfectionists who don't believe that they're perfectionists because they say, "How can I be a perfectionist if I don't do anything?" These are people who start lots of projects or new hobbies and never complete them because their work is never good enough, in their opinion. Since they feel that their work is never good enough, they believe that they themselves are never good enough. Perfectionists arrive at the top of one plateau, only to see that there is another plateau even higher that they need to get to next. They never arrive at their destination; they never achieve their goals. They can never have peace of mind or satisfaction in doing and/or completing a task. This is sometimes called *goal-vaulting*.

Perfectionism can be debilitating because it prevents happiness and contentment. Children who struggle with perfectionism often under-perform, under-sell themselves, and don't feel good even when they accomplish their goals. These are the kids who, when you say, "You're wonderful! Everyone thinks your great!" never agree with you because of their perfectionistic thinking, which tells them they are not good enough. They always notice that someone else is better than they are at everything, so that must mean they are failures.

I compare myself to others who are much more experienced than I am, and I become frustrated that I am not at the same level as they are.

~ 15-year-old warrior

Eating Disorders

Since we are including perfectionism in the list of "neigh-borhoods," this is a good time to discuss eating disorders, an issue related to perfectionism. Eating disorders are not often talked about in the anxiety realm; however, they are anxiety disorders too and can become dangerous and even life-threatening if they aren't treated. Eating disorders, such as anorexia, bulimia, and Body Dysmorphic Disorder, all involve an obsessive or intense need to have one's body look a certain way—generally more "perfect." This fear changes the way a person thinks, the way a person sees him- or herself in the mirror, and the way a person thinks about food and eating (and yes, eating disorders affect boys, too).

Many people slip into an eating disorder by channeling their anxiety into "being healthy." They become increasingly concerned with the negative effects that certain foods can have on their bodies, and they gradually restrict both the variety and quantity of the food they consume. This usually goes unnoticed by parents in the beginning because the child is receiving positive attention for not eating junk food and for paying attention to her health. Because the child isn't expressing a desire to be thin or perfect, they don't realize that the sudden interest in healthy eating can be a response to feeling out of control and anxious.

Anxiety can also affect how people experience their hunger signals. Some people overeat when they are anxious; other's can't eat at all. If your child is anxious and shows signs of restricting food, overeating, or exhibiting extreme concern with what foods she will and will not eat, please seek professional assistance as soon as possible. Eating disorders are serious, but the sooner they are assessed and treated, the less chance there is that they will negatively affect your child's life.

Individuals who are perfectionistic and high-achieving seem to be at greater risk for eating disorders. Recently, I met with a second grader who seemed advanced beyond her years. When we were going through her worry list so that we could tackle the Worry Monster, two of her five main worries were that she needed to dress fashionably so people would like her and that she had to look in the mirror several times a day to make sure she looked okay. This second grader looked like a fifth grader modeling for a fashion magazine! Without panicking and jumping to conclusions about her later developing an eating disorder, we calmly noted that we were in an at-risk "neighborhood" of what a lower-level fear of looking unfashionable can lead to later in some children if we don't put a damper on the Worry Monster now. This smart little girl was relieved to hear that there is such a thing as a Worry Monster that was making her think certain things that weren't actually true, even though she knew it was going be hard to fight those thoughts.

One last point: A common misconception is that parents "create" eating disorders by being perfectionistic and critical of their child's appearance and performance. While some parents do indeed misplace their anxiety onto their child in this way, the great majority of parents are *not* to blame for their child's eating disorder. The good news is that the same tools that work to defeat the Worry Monster will work to overcome an eating disorder as well.

Time to Relax and Breathe

Okay, I know what you may be thinking. Actually, I know what you may be worrying about. You are worrying that your child (and maybe you) has several of the anxiety issues listed in this chapter. I know this because it was exactly what I was thinking and worrying about when I was learning about all of this stuff. This is the same thing that happens to medical students when they study diseases: they start to think they have all of them and potentially get a little freaked out.

So listen up. I am going to impart a kernel of wisdom that I have learned over the years:

A problem is not a problem unless it's a problem.

Yes, I know, very profound. I will state it again: A problem is not a problem unless it's a problem.

Many children (and adults) have quirks. Remember playing the game "Step on a crack, and break your mamma's back?" How about always washing your hair before your body in the shower? Or always putting on your left sock before your right sock? And what if your child needs you to lie with her for exactly five minutes after reading two books before bed? Is any of this *really* a problem? Is it annoying? Is it a little bit quirky? Maybe. Everything we just talked about is based on a neighborhood, and there is a *huge* continuum in each neighborhood. The real concern is the degree that the anxiety is interfering with your child's ability to function and enjoy life. If anxiety is having a significant impact on joy, on the child's ability to function, and on being able to engage in and attend expected life events like school and social gatherings, then it probably is a problem. The tools in this book may be enough to help you address this problem. However, any time you are seriously concerned, please consult a professional. This self-help book is not intended to be a substitute for professional help when such help is needed.

Activity: What Neighborhood Are We In?

The following is a brief exercise to help you identify which general areas of anxiety your child's experiences tend to fall into. Read each description that follows, and write down which neighborhood or neighborhoods the child may be in. Answers are on page 46.

1. *Melissa has times when she feels like she is going to have a heart attack. She feels dizzy, can't catch her breath, and gets really scared. To her it feels like her chest is going to explode, and she gets more upset when people tell her that she is fine and that it's all in her head.*

2. *Lucas can't stop worrying about what others think of him. He worries that he doesn't have anything in common with the other kids. He is afraid to say anything because he is worried that he will say the wrong thing and that they will laugh at him.*

3. *Olivia doesn't like to go anywhere without her mother. She doesn't like to be left at school or at parties. She cries*

excessively when her mother has to leave, and she clings to her mother's leg. She thinks something bad will happen to her mother—for instance, her mother will get killed by a bad guy—while she is away.

4. *Jorge is never satisfied with his schoolwork. He is always focusing on what he could have done better. He doesn't try very many new things because he doesn't think he will be successful in eventually mastering new skills. If something doesn't come fairly easily right away, he avoids it. He usually thinks he is not good enough.*

5. *Paul is overly concerned about his body image and health. He runs two times a day and counts his calories. If he doesn't run two times or goes over his calorie intake goal, he feels bad about himself and is preoccupied until he runs extra miles the next day. Paul fears that if he doesn't carefully control every calorie he eats or expends, he will wake up with his life/body out of control.*

6. *Ami cries uncontrollably at times, but at other times she just seems to go blank. She gets tense when she has to get in a car and sometimes refuses. She says she can't stop thinking about the car accident she and her mom were in last year and how her mother was taken away in an ambulance.*

7. *Jeremy worries that something bad is going to happen to his family if he doesn't do certain things, like repeat numbers in his head and make sure that he touches everything two times. He feels funny if he doesn't do these things.*

8. *Autumn doesn't like going shopping at the mall anymore. She worries that she might have a panic attack and won't be able to escape. She also has started avoiding department stores and even the supermarket lately because she finds herself thinking, "It could happen there, too."*

9. *Marty hates going over bridges. He worries that the bridge will break and he'll fall into the water. He sometimes starts to*

have an "episode" when he knows he has to travel over a bridge that week. He gets light-headed and has trouble breathing.

10. *Ella has been waking up in the middle of the night feeling like she has a ton of bricks on her chest. She wakes up sweating and scared. Her legs feel numb, and her fists are clenched. These episodes seem to last for eternity, but in actuality they last about 10-15 minutes.*

11. *Marcus always seems to be worrying about something. He worries that people are talking about him behind his back. He worries that he will do poorly on tests. He worries that his parents will be unhappy with his grades and that he won't ever amount to anything.*

12. *Cassidy is obsessed with how she looks. She checks herself frequently in the mirror to reassure herself that she looks okay. She feels that she has to wear the latest clothes but is self-conscious when people comment on them. She wants them to think she looks great, but when they notice her, she feels like all they can see is how fat she is. And then she worries that they will remember her outfit, and she gets stressed about how she has to get another new outfit so she won't be teased for wearing the same thing twice.*

So now you know about how anxiety works in our brain and body and the types of anxiety that your child may experience. We are getting closer to putting together our battle plan for confronting the Worry Monster to fight him, capture him, tame him, and then banish him in order to make him leave and never come back. But first, let's take an even closer look at how anxiety can present itself when the Worry Monster is bullying your child.

What Does Anxiety Look Like?

So what does it look like? Think back to all of the those physical responses, or symptoms—about how excessive amounts of adrenaline cause blood to leave your child's main organs in order to make her into a "super fighter or flighter." Now let's put those symptoms into everyday scenarios.

Your child may complain of having headaches and/or stom-achaches in the morning before school, before a birthday party, before a test, and/or before bedtime. She may have trouble relaxing, have low energy, have trouble sleeping, have to go to the bathroom all the time, and/or may not have much of an appetite. There are plenty of other anxiety-related behaviors, too. These include nail biting, picking at one's skin, sucking on t-shirts, eating non-food items like napkins or ice, extreme clinginess, holding in one's bowels, and an excessive need for reassurance ("Did I do it right?" "Are you going to be okay?" "Am I going to be okay?"). Also, some children have tics, or nervous, repetitive behaviors like a facial twitch, that increase when they are anxious. If your child's behavior changes suddenly and dramatically within a few hours or days, it may mean that something is going on that could be related to anxiety.

Avoidance

In addition to physical complaints, your child may exhibit some challenging behaviors, too. A primary behavior is avoidance; in fact, avoidance is the Worry Monster's best friend. The more a child (or adult) avoids a certain situation, the stronger his or her worry and anxiety get.[16] It's that simple. We avoid what we don't like. If you don't like to fly, you take the extra time it takes to get to your destination by driving. If you don't like animals, you don't go to the zoo. If you're afraid of insects, you don't go outdoors very often. Avoidance is a natural human response. However, avoiding situations like this can get in the way of living a normal life. Children may also try to avoid going to school, talking to people, trying new things, taking a risk, and getting in front of people—all regular life activities. Avoiding things may also cause your child to quit something he loves, like music or sports, because he doesn't know how to cope with his fears surrounding the activity.

You will learn ways to help your child face and stare down the Worry Monster on the way to gaining victories over him. Avoiding an activity or a place only serves to reinforce the fear and make the Worry Monster stronger. For example, if your child refuses to go to birthday parties because he is afraid of what might happen, continuing to avoid parties only reinforces the notion that something bad might happen. Thus, avoidance helps the Worry Monster's lies seem true. Conversely, if your child actually went to some birthday parties and saw that nothing bad happened while he was there, he might see that his fears were unfounded.

Besides avoidance, children with anxiety are likely to experience a lot of crying, meltdowns, and disruptive behavior. This is an important group of symptoms to think about because it is easily misunderstood. Early in my career, I found myself sitting at school meetings after completing comprehensive assessments of challenging kids who were seen as "behavior problems" at their schools. Due to their acting out, they were presumed to have a behavior disorder. These kids, however, had something else important that was gong on besides their acting out: they had anxiety. Their anxiety was showing itself in their disruptive behavior. Think of it as a variation of the "fight or flight" response.

The fight response to fear doesn't necessarily mean that we start hitting people. It does mean that we act out our adrenalin rush in some way other than "fight" or "flight." These children couldn't articulate their fears, and so they were reacting behaviorally because their amygdala, or their emotional brain, was overriding their thinking brain. They weren't able to think; they were just responding by refusing, running away, ripping up paper, hitting, pushing, and/or screaming. When we give children like these tools to use other than

acting out negative behaviors, their behavioral symptoms decrease and often go away altogether.

> *It's weird. Some kids melt down both at school and at home. Some just melt down at school, and some just melt down at home. I try not to show my feelings at school. I wait until I get home.*
>
> ~ eight-year-old warrior

Whether your child is experiencing strong physiological responses related to excessive adrenaline (stomach pain, headaches, chest tightening) or is refusing to participate in an activity to avoid having those uncomfortable feelings, tell him that anxious and uncomfortable feelings *always* go away eventually—and keep repeating that. Even the really bad feelings *always* go away—he just needs to "ride the wave" until they do. It doesn't feel like that would be possible when it is happening, but they *always* do. Sometimes we just need to help our child get through the bad feelings. Surviving the Worry Monster's attack is a victory in itself.

Please remember that kids often do not have the emotional vocabulary and/or insight to tell you what is going on. All they may know is that they are scared and feel awful. The way they show this may be in very difficult or even deviant behaviors. It is our job as parents, and as professionals who do this work, to pick apart the puzzle and help uncover the sneaky and powerful effects of the Worry Monster at work.

Things to Remember

- ✔ There are several different types of anxiety that can affect your child.

- ✔ A problem is not a problem unless it's a problem. The amount of distress the anxiety causes your child, as well as how much it impairs her ability to engage in daily responsibilities and activities, is what matters.

✔ Your child may express her worry or fear in physical symptoms or behaviors or both. The symptoms and behaviors can be quiet ones, or they can be loud.

✔ Avoidance is a common behavior when your child is scared. She is managing her anxiety by refusing to put herself in certain situations, but this behavior is ultimately not helpful.

✔ Anxious feelings *always* go away eventually, though it's hard to convince a child (or an adult) of that.

Things to Do

✔ Ask yourself which area(s) of anxiety your child may be in.

✔ If you think your child would understand and benefit, teach her about the different kinds of anxiety.

✔ Ask your child if any of the different kinds of anxiety sound or feel familiar. Sometimes it helps to give the monster a name.

✔ Think about how your child may express her anxiety with physical symptoms or behaviors.

✔ Ask your child how the Worry Monster makes her feel.

✔ Ask your child what the Worry Monster makes her do.

Neighborhood Activity Answers

1. Panic Attacks	7. Obsessive-Compulsive Disorder
2. Social Phobia	8. Agoraphobia
3. Separation Anxiety	9. Specific Phobia, Panic Attacks
4. Perfectionism	10. Panic Attacks
5. Eating Disorder, Perfectionism	11. Generalized Anxiety
6. Post-Traumatic Stress Disorder	12. Social Phobia, Perfectionism

CHAPTER 4

Cognitive Model of Anxiety

When we fill our thoughts with right things, the wrong ones have no room to enter.

~ Joyce Meyer

The cognitive model of anxiety has become a widely accepted and effective approach to understanding and dealing with anxiety. Going back to our brains, our thinking (or *cognition*) originates primarily from our frontal lobes—the front portion of our brain behind our forehead and eyes. The reason we humans are "masters of the universe" is because we have very large frontal lobes that allow us to problem solve—more so than any other species. Thus, it is helpful to teach kids to use their large frontal lobes to overpower their small, almond-size amygdala and to explain that they have way more neurons in their frontal lobes than they do in their amygdala. They can understand that they need their amygdala to stay alive, but much of the time when it is "turned on" they don't need it to be on because they are merely performing, going someplace new, or trying a new skill, not surviving!

Thoughts Cause Feelings

Cognitive theorists teach us that our thoughts, behaviors, and emotions are all connected. So if we change our thinking, it leads to changes in our behaviors and feelings. Similarly, if we change our behaviors, it leads to changes in our thinking and feelings.

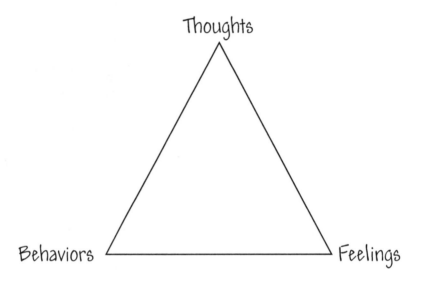

The main concept in the cognitive model of anxiety (the thinking model of anxiety) is that our thoughts are always responsible for our feelings. Our irrational and worried thoughts are almost always exaggerations of what could be or what might be, and they usually sound like this: "What if I...?" "What if you...?" "What if they...?" "What's going to happen to her if she doesn't...?" "How am I ever going to...?" "What will people think if...?" These are all future-based thoughts that trigger our amygdala to make us feel uncomfortable, worried, and scared.

How the Worry Monster Works

So here is how the Worry Monster works. A child has a distressing thought: "Oh no, my mom is going to leave, and she might never come back!" This is not a comfortable thought when you're a child. The child's amygdala goes off, and her inner alarm bells start ringing. Physiological responses quickly follow: she has an upset stomach and tightness in her chest, feels light-headed, and experiences tingling in her fingers. She then has even more thoughts about how everything is awful and what additional bad things are going to happen after the first bad things start happening.

All of this is going on inside her head—and you can't read her mind. But all of a sudden she says something like, "I'm not going to that party," or "I'm not going to that school." And just like that, your child may be flopping around on the ground, having a tantrum, crying, screaming, hiding, and/or being behaviorally disruptive, rude, and/or oppositional. These symptoms are all responses to how she is feeling: scared, worried, and anxious. The Worry Monster is definitely messing with her. Rather than getting angry with your child for her unpleasant behaviors (which may be wreaking havoc with your plans to get out the door to where you need to go), you need to realize that your child mostly needs your compassionate support to help her fight the Worry Monster.

The classic and common example is when you are running late to an activity, and you tell your child a new piece of information, such as that it's a dress-up party, that there are going to be more people there than usual, or that she may have to stay a little longer than usual. With an anxious child, these "simple" additional details can easily trigger a meltdown and defiance. It is important to try to take a few breaths and realize that although you wish your child could more easily go with the flow, the new information has made her worried about something, like who is going to be there, who she might have to talk to, and what people will think of her. As you well know, the frequent parent response of getting mad at the meltdown (which I still do more than I would like, even though I know better!) usually doesn't help and only makes things worse. You are still late, your child is still upset, you are mad, and when it's all over, you feel like a "bad" parent.

Here Comes Adrenaline!

Every time the Worry Monster gives your child a worrisome or scary thought, the child's amygdala activates and sends a message through his body that says: "Get me more adrenaline, quick!" For example, if your child is going to take a test and thinks, "Oh my gosh! I'm going to forget everything that I studied last night," squirt goes the adrenaline, flooding through the body. "Oh my gosh! I'm going to *fail* this test," and his body squirts more adrenaline. "Oh no, my parents are going to be *so mad* at me," and another squirt, even more adrenaline. "I'm not going get on the honor roll," new squirt. "Oh my gosh! I'm going to have to miss my…," squirt, squirt, squirt; it just keeps going and going and going. To dramatize this, Dr. Liebgold actually has used a squirt gun in his Phobese™ classes to show kids and parents that every time we have a worrisome thought, more adrenaline is squirting through our bodies.[17]

Taking on the Worry Monster

So how do we tame this unwanted, bothersome Worry Monster? Taming the Worry Monster is a team effort. It's a parent-child effort, it's a family effort, and we may even need to get our child's teachers or grandparents on board to help us get rid of him. As one family I know put it, fighting the Worry Monster requires everyone, including siblings, to be "all in." It takes commitment, resolve, persistence, patience, and courage.

A key principle in helping children overcome their worry and fear is to help them face it down. We can't let them avoid it because then the Worry Monster becomes more firmly rooted and bigger and stronger. But each time we face the Worry Monster, he gets smaller and less powerful. We need to remember that it takes a lot of courage for children to become warriors and to face their fears and worries. That is why we need to give them not only the tools to fight the Worry Monster, but also praise for each of their successes in facing their fears. We need to be patient with them. It is critical that we teach them about how the Worry Monster works, how their brain and their body work, and how they are reacting to the Worry Monster in very human ways; that way they understand that they are "normal" and not "weird." There is nothing wrong with them. Many other kids and adults have worries, just like they do.

We have to help children face their fears—even legitimately scary ones. We have to help them harness the power of their big frontal lobes over their little yet strong amygdala. We need to teach them to use their bigger thinking brain to overpower their smaller emotional brain. We need to teach them that the Worry Monster is telling them lies to make them scared, and they can learn to laugh at the Worry Monster and tell him to take a hike!

Things to Remember

✔ Our worrisome thoughts trigger our amygdala to release adrenaline.

✔ Too much adrenaline makes us feel scared and gets our bodies ready to fight or flee.

✔ Our thoughts affect our emotions and behaviors.

✔ The more we think worrisome thoughts, the more adrenaline is released, and the more scared we feel.

✔ Changing our thoughts changes our emotions and behavior—and sends the Worry Monster away.

✔ Helping your child to face his fears is critical for making them go away.

Things to Do

✔ Teach your child that the Worry Monster tells him worrisome and scary thoughts that trigger his amygdala to make him feel scared.

✔ Teach your child that with every scary thought comes more adrenaline and more scary feelings.

✔ Tell your child that if he can change his thinking, his amygdala will not go on, he will feel better, and the Worry Monster will go away.

✔ Tell him that you are going to help him get rid of the Worry Monster and that, together, you are way stronger than that old monster is.

✔ Tell him that you are going to help him face his fears in a way that isn't too scary, and when he does this, he will feel stronger, more confident, and less scared.

CHAPTER 5

Thinking Errors

You wouldn't worry so much about what others think of you if you realized how seldom they do.

~ Eleanor Roosevelt

As we have discussed, the Worry Monster places worrisome and irrational thoughts into our brains to make us feel worried and scared. These faulty and irrational thinking patterns are sometimes referred to as thinking errors, or "stinking thinking." Becoming aware of the types of thinking errors in general, and your child's thinking errors in particular, can help you better understand the basis of her worries, as well as how her (erroneous) thinking is resulting in her uncomfortable feelings. In other words, what is the Worry Monster telling your child to make her worried and scared?

This chapter discusses the most commonly identified thinking errors. They include:[18]

✔ Catastrophizing
✔ All or nothing thinking
✔ Filtering
✔ Selective attention
✔ Magnifying
✔ Shoulds

✔ Mind reading
✔ Personalizing
✔ Overgeneralizing
✔ Probability overestimation

Catastrophizing

A person who visualizes that disaster will strike at any time, who thinks that the worst possibilities are going to happen, and who feels like she won't be able to handle it when they do happen is catastrophizing. "If don't do well on this spelling test, I'm never going to get into college!" "I will never have any friends!" "Mom is five minutes late already—I'm sure she's gotten into a horrible car accident! How will my life change if I don't have a mom?" To others, the catastrophizing is clearly unreasonable, but to the individual battling such thinking, the thoughts seem certain outcomes to the situation at hand.

All or Nothing Thinking

This kind of thinking is also called black and white thinking because there is no middle ground, no gray area. It's an inflexible and irrational style of thinking because it implies that no middle ground exists between extremes; it is "always" or "never." It is extreme thinking—that we either have to do things perfectly or have failed, that people either like us or hate us. We often see examples of all or nothing thinking in reference to a child's grades, as in an A means success, but a B or any other grade is failure. Getting a B, particularly in a subject that is hard for a student, may be a blessing in disguise, since it can force the child to see that the world didn't come crashing down just because he didn't bring home all A's.

Filtering

Filtering means focusing on the negative aspects of a situation while ignoring the positive parts. As an example, let's say that your child got invited to a party she very much wanted to go to, but when she gets home, she only focuses on the times at the party when she didn't feel included. Or even though your child had a lot of fun at the school picnic, she only thinks about the part of the picnic when the kid in front of her took the last bag of Doritos and she had to have plain potato chips. Filtering can also be described as "bad bookkeeping," in which one bad thing outweighs all of the good things in a situation.

Selective Attention

Selective attention is similar to filtering. It is when a person looks for aspects of a situation that are consistent with and confirm his beliefs about something while at the same time ignoring information that goes against what he knows to be true. A child might say, "My coach thinks I didn't play well and that I need to work harder," when in fact the coach actually made several positive comments and offered constructive criticism about only one play the child made. Or a child might say, "I can't believe I missed that question! How stupid can I be?!" in response to missing one out of 100 questions on a test.

Magnifying

When a child magnifies an event or an issue, he is blowing it out of proportion or making it seem bigger and worse than it really is—for example, "I made a mistake, and now everyone is going to laugh at me every time they see me," or, "I failed the test, and now my future is ruined!" or, "When I was giving my presentation to the class, I dropped my pen, and now everyone thinks I am clumsy and stupid. And they won't want me to play kickball with them ever again." Intense children are particularly likely to magnify.

Shoulds

This thinking error refers to "rules" that some people have about how things should be. The rules might be about their home, their school, or the entire world, and they are identifiable when your child uses words like *should*, *have to*, and *must* to explain how things "should" and "must" be. "I should not make mistakes." "I have to always do things perfectly." "I must always get 100% on tests." "I must know more than everyone else." Also, "would haves" and "could haves" similarly create uncomfortable feelings in children that can make them feel despondent for hours, days, months, or even years. "I would have gotten an A if the teacher hadn't put in a trick question." "I could have been the top speller, but I got a really hard word." "I could have gotten first place, but I let Jason win." Watch out for "shoulda…woulda…coulda…"!

Mind Reading

Mind reading is what a person does when she thinks she knows what others are thinking—particularly when it comes to what they are thinking about *her*. Some kids always assume that others are thinking negatively or badly about them. "They think I'm stupid." "They don't want me to play with them." "I can tell you think I'm a bad singer, Mom. You keep saying nice things, but you don't really mean it." "I can tell you're mad because you keep reading the paper and ignoring me." Usually, these kinds of assumptions also involve an imaginary audience—that is, the child is absolutely sure that everyone is watching and will know the mistake she has made.

Personalizing

Personalizing is what people do when they assume that something that happened was because of them. A child (or adult) who personalizes makes everything about herself, when most things actually have nothing to do with her. For example, your child's friend cancels plans to get together, and your daughter assumes, "She doesn't like me anymore." In fact, her friend actually canceled because her parents decided that the family needed to go check on a relative who was just involved in an accident. The situation has nothing to do with your daughter, but she assumes that it does.

Overgeneralizing

Looking at one situation or incident and thinking that it will always be that way or happen that way again is overgeneralizing. Once something happens, the child assumes that it will always happen the same way each time. "I didn't get invited to Bryan's party. I'm never going to get invited to anyone's party again!" "I got a C on that test. I'm just stupid, and I'm never going to do well on a test again." *Always, never, only, every, all, none, everyone, no one,* and *nothing* are danger words. Use them with care!

Probability Overestimation

Probability overestimation is similar to magnifying and catastrophizing—it's worrying about something that actually has a slim chance of occurring. If a person looks at the actual data, the thing she fears is easily proven to be unlikely to happen. However, even the small and extremely remote possibility of the accident or incident occurring is scary. "The plane could crash, and I will die," "I might get kidnapped," "My parents could get killed," and "A meteor might fall on me" are all examples of probability overestimation with catastrophic thinking. These events rarely occur, but the child reacts to them as though they are very likely to happen. Another example of probability overestimation is when a child who has never failed a test before is afraid that she will fail the next test, even though she has no foundation for her thinking.

Additional Thinking Errors

Two additional common thinking errors are "What if...?" and "What will people think...?"[19] Think about how many times you have heard your child (or yourself) say those phrases and how they make your child doubt himself and worry about the future.

"What if...?"

The "What ifs" may be the most single powerful trick the Worry Monster uses. The Worry Monster can put a "What if" in front of anything:

- ✔ "What if I don't get the part I want in the play?"
- ✔ "What if I don't get on the team?"
- ✔ "What if I do badly on the test?"
- ✔ "What if I don't get invited to the party?"
- ✔ "What if I get scared and want to come home early?"

And the list goes on and on and on. Any time you hear your child say, "What if…?" it means the Worry Monster is probably at work. Knowing how the Worry Monster uses the "What if…?" strategy against her, a brave 13-year-old warrior I know now says, "What if? Whatever!" and just dismisses the Worry Monster like he doesn't matter to her one bit. And it works!

"What will people think…?"

"What will people think…?" is a perfect companion to "What if…?" With both of these tactics, the Worry Monster has the fear market cornered. Once he tells your child about all of the possible things that can go wrong with her life using the "What ifs…?" he then follows up with "And what will people think…?"

- ✔ "What will people think of me if I forget my lines?"
- ✔ "What will people think if I strike out?"
- ✔ "What will people think if I don't get an A?"
- ✔ "What will people think if I'm the only one not invited?"
- ✔ "What will people think if I go home early?"

The Short List

If the sheer volume of thinking errors listed in this chapter seems overwhelming, I have a condensed version for you. Drs. David Barlow and Michelle Craske, international authorities on anxiety and panic, have summarized them all into two main categories: (1) jumping to conclusions about negative events, and (2) blowing things out of proportion.[20] You likely will find that these categories cover many, if not all, of your child's (and your own) worried thinking.

Are you starting to get annoyed with the Worry Monster? I certainly am. All he does is make our children (and us) miserable! And he does this by simply muddling up our children's thinking so that their alarm bells go off, their body gets flooded with adrenalin, and—no surprise—they feel awful. Enough is enough!

Activity: What Are Your Child's (and Your) Thinking Patterns?

This activity is designed to help you become familiar with the types of thinking errors your child may engage in. You may find that he uses the same few thinking errors repeatedly or that he has a variety of worrisome thinking patterns. List the thinking error associated with each statement. You may do this activity by yourself or with your child (if you have already explained the thinking errors in this chapter to him). Answers are on page 61.

1. *They think I'm stupid.*
2. *I never do things right. I always blow it!*
3. *I never get picked to be a partner.*
4. *I shouldn't make any mistakes.*
5. *What will people think if I mess up?*
6. *I know the teacher said I did a good job, but she corrected two of my answers, so she really didn't mean it.*
7. *I can't go on the fieldtrip without you. What if I get lost and they leave without me?*
8. *What if burglars break into my house and take me?*
9. *They wouldn't let me lead the line walking into the museum, so the whole fieldtrip was ruined.*
10. *I know she said she liked what I was wearing, but she was laughing with Julie after she looked at me.*
11. *If I don't get a good grade on this, I will never get into college.*
12. *She cancelled the party because she didn't want me there.*

So how did you do? Many of the statements could fall into several categories of thinking errors. The main point is that you ultimately help your child learn to identify his thinking errors in order to show him how the Worry Monster tricks him into being worried and scared. I know this sounds simple, but helping your child be aware of how the Worry Monster tells him lies to make him scared is one of the key strategies in combating that old ogre. Look out Worry Monster; you are going to become weaker and weaker until you totally lose your power!

Things to Remember

- ✔ Our worrisome thoughts are always responsible for feelings of worry and fear.

- ✔ The Worry Monster uses several different kinds of thinking tricks to make us worry and feel scared.

- ✔ People tend to have a few "favorite" thinking errors that often make them worry or feel scared.

- ✔ The Worry Monster is *always* lying to you!

Things to Do

- ✔ Teach your child about the different types of thinking errors.

- ✔ Help your child identify which thinking errors the Worry Monster makes her think.

- ✔ Identify your own thinking errors.

- ✔ Share your thinking errors with your child to help her see that the Worry Monster gets to you too, and you both are going to work on making him go away.

- ✔ Tell your child that the Worry Monster is *always* telling her lies.

Thinking Patterns Activity Answers

1. Mind Reading

2. All or Nothing Thinking, Magnifying, Overgeneralizing

3. All or Nothing Thinking, Magnifying, Overgeneralizing, Personalizing

4. Shoulds

5. "What will people think...?"

6. Selective Attention

7. Catastrophizing, "What if...?"

8. Catastrophizing, Probability Overestimation, "What if...?"

9. Filtering

10. Selective Attention, Personalizing

11. Catastrophizing

12. Personalizing

CHAPTER 6

Cognitive (Thinking) Interventions

You don't have to control your thoughts. You just have to stop letting them control you.

~ Dan Millman

Now we are getting to the really exciting part: the part where we start to take charge of the Worry Monster by using his own sneaky strategies against him! He hates it when we realize that he is there, and even more when we know how he works. Unfortunately, most people never learn the simple fact that our *thoughts* determine our *emotions* and our *behaviors*.

This is such a simple concept; it has been around since at least the 1960s.[21] It is time to get this concept into our educational curriculum, don't you think? More importantly, at least for the moment, it is time to get this concept into your home to help your child fight off the Worry Monster. It is time for your child to learn that when she is feeling scared (and also very sad or depressed), she has a particular type of thinking that is responsible for her awful, anxious feelings and corresponding emotions and behaviors.

The first thing you can do to start the process of chasing the Worry Monster away is to ask your child, "What are you thinking right now?" Older kids usually can answer this question easily enough, and so can some young, insightful children. Other children may be either too young or lack the insight and awareness to identify their thinking. Even so, it is still important to try to help these children learn to identify their thinking. However, if they are not yet able, don't worry. They can still chase the Worry Monster away with the strategies we will discuss soon. People of all ages, not just kids, often have trouble identifying what they are thinking and feeling. This is why we have come up with multiple ways to successfully make the Worry Monster go away and stay away.

Four Steps

The approach we will take is really very simple. You are going to become a detective with your child in order to figure out what the Worry Monster is telling him and making him think. You may ask your child if he can be a detective to discover the clues that the Worry Monster leaves for him. The way to do this is to help your child learn to follow four simple steps to chase the Worry Monster away:

- ✔ *Identify the thought*: "What am I thinking about? What is my thinking error? Is it that I'm scared I'm going to fail the test?"

- ✔ *Challenge the thought*: "Is it true that I always fail? Do I have evidence to support that I always fail?"

- ✔ *Modify the thought*: "The test is going to be hard, but I am prepared. I usually get nervous before math tests but generally do pretty well."

- ✔ *Replace the thought*: "I am prepared. I will try my best and will do fine."

In this simple four-step model, your child (with your help) will engage in a short process of scientific inquiry. While thinking about his thinking, he will effectively turn down the volume of his small amygdala (emotional brain) and turn up the power of his big frontal lobes (thinking brain). Thus, the warning signals from his amygdala will decrease, the adrenaline surges will go away, and his blood will stay in his brain. Keeping his blood in his brain is what he needs to fight the Worry Monster.

Until your child learns to go through this four-step process on his own, he will need you to talk him through it (over and over). You will ask your child simple questions like:

> *What are you thinking? What is the Worry Monster telling you? Is that thought really true? What is the evidence? Can you prove it? Can you prove that something's going to happen to me? Can you prove that you are going to fail the test? Can you prove that no one's going to like you? Or invite you to their party? Or that you'll be kidnapped? Or that something else bad will happen? What happened last time? Oh, Jeremy was mean to you? Well, what about Sophie and Ariel and Karl? They weren't? Oh, okay, so one of the four people wasn't so nice to you. Did your thoughts say that everyone is going to be mean to you? So maybe the Worry Monster was tricking you? Hmm, interesting. So maybe it's more accurate to say that while it is possible that someone will be mean to you, most people are usually nice.*

When you start to go through these exercises of inquiry regularly with your child, you will be helping him to understand his common thinking errors and his thinking patterns in general. We all have customary thinking errors, and you'll get to know your child's favorite ones—or, more accurately, the Worry Monster's favorite ones. The Worry Monster gives these worrisome thoughts to us, and we need to challenge them:

> *How can we look at this differently? When you go to the party, most of the kids will probably like you, but maybe one or two might not be very nice. How awful is that really? Isn't that normal? Have you had any other experiences like that where you thought people were going to be mean and they weren't? So maybe you can say that you think you're*

going to have a pretty good time at the party, even though maybe one or two kids might not be so nice to you.

As you can imagine, helping your child to change his thinking will result in different feelings and different behaviors. He will have negative and distressing feelings if he's thinking, "Everyone hates me," "I'm going to fail," "My teacher is going to be mad at me," "My parents are going to ground me," "I'm never going to amount to anything," "I'm too fat," or "I'm stupid." But your child will have more positive and less distressing feelings if he learns to replace that kind of thinking with thoughts that are healthier and more adaptive: "I have friends, which means some people like me," "I studied for the test, so I probably will do okay," "My teacher just wants me to do my best," "I can handle it if my parents ground me; it's not the end of the world," "I'm going to take one day at a time," "I am fine the way I am," or "I don't like making mistakes, but they happen sometimes." These healthier, more positive thoughts are the thoughts the Worry Monster most hates. He's counting on us believing his lying, sneaky, mean, and manipulative thoughts, no matter how ridiculous they may be.

This is all we need to do to help our children with their thinking: *identify* it, *challenge* it, *modify* it, and then *replace* it. It's a four-step model that you practice over and over again until your child says to you, "I know! Okay! Okay! I get it already!" When you get there, you're done. You've annoyed your child to the point at which he's not anxious anymore!

Here is an example of a warrior named Adam. It demonstrates how Adam's father helped him work through his worries by using this four-step approach to change his thinking. Adam was new to this approach, so he wasn't able to talk himself through his fear yet.

Adam, age eight, doesn't want to go to soccer tryouts, even though he loves soccer and his friends will be there. He starts to protest several days before, saying, "I am not going, and you can't make me." His father is used to this kind of anxious response from Adam.

Father: *It sounds like the Worry Monster is visiting you again.*

Adam: *No, he's not. I just don't want to go.*

Father: *Hmm, let's see. I know you love soccer and want to be on your friends' team again. I'm guessing the Worry Monster is trying to trick you. Remember when he did that to you before last year's tryouts?*

Adam: *Yeah, it wasn't as bad as I thought it was going to be.*

Father: *Where is the Worry Monster making you feel bad in your body? Is he making your heart beat fast, giving you a stomachache, or making you feel dizzy?*

Adam: *He's making my chest feel funny, and I can't breathe right.*

Father: *Remember what we learned about the survival response? When the Worry Monster tells us scary things, it makes our body feel like we need to fight or run. What might the Worry Monster be telling you about this tryout? I'm guessing he might be saying something like, "What if you make a mistake? What will people think? People are going to be watching you." Is he saying something like that?*

Adam: *He's telling me that I might not know where to go when I get there, and I might forget how to kick and dribble.*

Father: *I figured he was telling you something like that because I know how much you like soccer, so it would have to be something pretty bad for you to not want to go try out for the team. You know how the Worry Monster tells you lies to make your worried and scared. Now that we know what he's saying to you, what's the evidence that what he's saying is true? What can you tell him to make him stop? How can you think differently?*

Adam: *I can tell myself that I know where to go because I've been there before. I can also tell him that I know he's lying because I play soccer a lot and know how to play.*

Father: *Do you feel scared when you think those thoughts?*

Adam: *No, but he makes me feel bad when he tells me the other stuff.*

Father: *I know. How about we do this: Tryouts are still a few days away. So during that time, you tell me when he's making you feel bad, and then we can talk about the lies he's telling you and talk back to him with the truth. Do you think we can try that?*

Adam: *Okay. We can do that. You're still going to stay the whole time I'm at tryouts, right?*

Father: *Right.*

Adam eventually learned to recognize when the Worry Monster was visiting, and he became good at identifying the worrisome thoughts that were making him scared. He also learned to challenge his thinking on his own. He talked to his dad about it after he made the Worry Monster go away, as well as when the Worry Monster was being a super-bully and wouldn't go away. Adam and his father became a good team united to defeat the Worry Monster!

Additional Cognitive Strategies

Positive Self-Talk

In addition to the simple four-step model, a great way of helping to defeat the Worry Monster is through positive self-talk. Positive self-talk is one of the oldest sure-fire strategies around. One well-known example of it is in the children's book *The Little Engine that Could*, in which the small engine said, "I think I can, I think

I can, I think I can" as she delivered toys to the girls and boys on the other side of the mountain. The Little Engine actually predates cognitive theory, but it's the kind of self-talk that encourages us and makes us strong.

Here's another example of positive self-talk.[22] Imagine your child walking down the hallway at night in the dark saying to herself, "I'm not afraid, I'm not afraid, I'm not afraid, I'm not afraid." This simple strategy works because your child is using her thinking brain to turn off her amygdala. If she did not take over the command center in her brain, her amygdala would choose a different repetitive thought to play, which likely would be something like, "I'm going to be attacked by a bogey man, I am going to be attacked by a bogey man, I am going to be attacked by a bogey man!" I know; it sounds way too simple, but it works. It's another strategy for teaching kids that they have great brains that they *can* have control over. They can use their thinking brain to change the way they feel and chase the Worry Monster away!

> *I always get afraid when I walk into a new situation where I don't know who is going to be there. My heart starts pounding, and I start to feel a little dizzy. I try to remember to say the same thing to myself over and over until my heart starts to slow down. Lately, I say, "Nothing bad is going to happen, nothing bad is going to happen, nothing bad is going to happen."*
>
> *I am getting used to the idea that the Worry Monster comes to visit me at certain times. One of his favorite times is when I read the first question of a test. If I don't know the answer right away, he tells me, "You are going to fail." I have learned to say back to him, "I will be fine." I say it over and over and over until I am able to focus on the test question instead of him.*
>
> 12-year-old warrior

Worry Time

Scheduling "worry time" is a great way to put some boundaries on a child's worry and thus help her to feel more in control of her feelings of anxiety.[23] It also allows her to not get bogged down by the Worry Monster because she can tell herself, "I don't have to worry about that now; worry time is from 7:45 to 8:00 tonight." Worry time not only reduces worrying during the day, but it also reduces worry overall because kids often forget what they were worrying about earlier in the day.

While we don't want our kids to worry, it is important to tell them that worrying is something that is a part of life, so making time for it takes away the immediate intensity of the worry and allows for proactive problem solving. For example, if your child is worrying that she won't have time to finish something or to manage all of her obligations, she can train herself to solve her scheduling issues during her worry time later that day. This allows her to reduce her worry in the moment so that she can focus on the task at hand.

Worry Box

I have seen great results when children create a "worry box." The worry box, which can be an artistic creation from something as simple as a shoebox, becomes a place where a child puts pieces of paper on which he has written down his worries so that he no longer has to think about them. Some kids put their worry box under their beds; some put it in the closet. This strategy gives children actual physical space between their worries and themselves. It is also fun—and useful—to look in the worry box with your child every once in awhile to see if the things he put in there were worth worrying about. Of course, only do this for the things that are no longer worries or are small worries, as we certainly don't want to make the Worry Monster right! And if the Worry Monster was right that something bad happened...well, guess what? Your child survived it!

"And then what?"

I am a big fan of the "And then what?" strategy. Here's how it works. After your child has a worrisome or scary thought, she asks herself, "And then what?" It goes like this: "I'm worried that I'll get a bad grade on my test. *And then what?* I will get a bad grade in my class. *And then what?* My parents will be mad. *And then what?* I'll get grounded. *And then what?* I won't be able to see my friends. *And then what?* I will miss out on a fun sleepover." And it keeps going and going. You also can do this with your child, with you asking, "And then what?" after each conclusion she draws.

Next, you and your child will take on the role of detectives to determine if any of what your child said is actually true. Does one bad test performance equal a bad grade in a class? Will she really be ground if she gets a bad test grade or a bad grade in a class (when she is trying)? Will she really not be able to see her friends? When we investigate the truth of each situation, we often discover that the conclusions our child is drawing are good examples of catastrophizing, magnifying, or other thinking errors. When our child recognizes this, it can help her to reset her expectations of what would really occur if the bad thing she's worried about actually happened. In this way, the "And then what?" technique helps uncover lies the Worry Monster is telling your child. In addition, your child will discover that she can handle most of the things the Worry Monster tells her, like missing a sleepover. So she missed it. So what?

Planning for Worst-Case Scenarios

Planning for worst-case scenarios is a good way to help your child prepare for what he is worrying about. As you have learned, people often have fears that they just accept instead of challenging how true they are. They also tend to feel that they won't be able to handle bad situations if and when they happen. Planning for worst-case scenarios means helping your child think through how he will handle a situation if it were to come true. For example, I know a 10-year-old girl, Paige, who was worried that she wouldn't get the lead part in the play she was auditioning for, and it was very important to her. We used the worst-case scenario to work through this:

Paige: *I'm worried I won't get the lead part that I've been practicing for. Everyone expects me to get it, and I'll be disappointed and embarrassed if I don't get it.*

Me: *What will happen if you don't get the part?*

Paige: *I'll probably get another important role, just not the lead.*

Me: *What will happen then?*

Paige: *People may be a little surprised, but I'll work hard at my role and do the best I can.*

Me: *How will that be for you?*

Paige: *I guess it will be okay. I can try for the lead in the next play.*

Me: *So not getting the lead it is not as bad as you thought?*

Paige: *No, I guess not. It just felt like it would be.*

The worst-case scenario approach is another way of questioning the Worry Monster's lies, but your child's reasonable and rational thoughts are more powerful!

Things to Remember

- ✔ Our thoughts determine our emotions and behaviors.
- ✔ The Worry Monster tells us irrational and worrisome thoughts to make us feel worried and scared.
- ✔ We need to identify our thinking to help uncover what the Worry Monster is telling us.
- ✔ Not all kids, or even adults, can identify their thinking.
- ✔ We can help our kids be detectives with their thoughts and ask them if the thoughts are actually true.
- ✔ Changing our thoughts and replacing them with more reasonable ones turns our amygdala down and makes the Worry Monster weak and powerless.
- ✔ There are several different strategies to choose from to fight the Worry Monster.

Things to Do

- ✔ Remind your child that worrisome thoughts, given to her by the Worry Monster, make her feel bad.

- ✔ Ask your child what she feels and where she feels it when she is feeling scared.

- ✔ Ask your child what she is thinking when she gets scared or worried.

- ✔ Give your child suggestions about what the Worry Monster may be telling her to make her worried or scared.

- ✔ Help your child come up with and practice self-talk that makes her feel confident and strong.

- ✔ Teach your child about worry time.

- ✔ Make a worry box with your child.

- ✔ Ask your child "And then what?" to help her identify realistic consequences for the things she worries about.

- ✔ Help your child plan for worst-case scenarios so she can see that even if things don't go the way she would like, everything will still be okay.

CHAPTER 7

Mindfulness - Based Interventions

The mind is everything. What you think, you become.

~ Buddha

I would like to introduce you to mindfulness-based strategies for fighting the Worry Monster. Although mindfulness has been practiced in the Eastern world for thousands of years, the Western world has only recently embraced it as effective for fighting anxiety and depression and cultivating a state of inner well-being. Jon Kabat-Zinn's book *Full Catastrophe Living*,[24] a highly influential work in the fields of both physical and mental health, teaches people to use mindfulness techniques to reduce chronic pain, anxiety, and depression. Mindfulness-based strategies are wonderful to infuse into the cognitive strategies discussed in the last chapter, too.

Mindfulness strategies come from Eastern philosophies, from both Buddhist and Zen ways of thinking. The Dalai Lama, spiritual leader of Tibet and a very wise man, pointed out that people who live in the past tend to be depressed because it already happened and there's nothing they can do about it, and people who live in the future tend to be anxious because it hasn't happened yet and there's nothing they can do about it.[25] So if living in and thinking about the *past* makes us depressed, and living in and thinking about the *future* makes us anxious, then the goal is to try to live in the *present*. Simple to say, yet challenging to do.

Staying in the Present

In my own life, and through the experiences of many of my clients, I have learned that staying in the present is the single most powerful technique for keeping the Worry Monster at bay. Here's why: if we live in the present, everything is fine because most of the time, things are fine (or manageable enough) right at this moment. For example, right now, I am engaged in writing this book, and now you are engaged in reading it. We are both hopefully engaged in something meaningful. You are learning about ways to help your child fight the Worry Monster and are focusing on these words at this moment. Everything is fine right now.

But now let's decide that it's time to start worrying—let's start to worry together. On your mark, get set, GO! Let's start worrying about our bills, our career, our unfinished projects, our kids, our parents, and our friends. Maybe our credit card bills are too high, or we might get a call from our child's teacher this week about "a problem at school." Maybe we are totally buried in emails at work and feel we may never catch up. The list goes on and on and on when it comes to what we may choose to worry about right this second—and none of it has happened yet. Sorry to do that to you— to get your adrenalin going like that. I just needed to make the point about how easy it is to slide into worry about the future. Let's end that planned worrying exercise and come back to this book and the words you are reading in front of your eyes. Bring your focus back now to the present moment where everything was, and still is, fine.

Are you back to the present moment? It may take some effort. It can be hard to dial our amygdalas down and allow time for our blood to return to our brain where it belongs. Give yourself some time. Take some deep breaths, and return to these words when you are ready. Now, try to come back to the present moment where we are focused on doing our best and learning how to focus on the *present*. The Dalai Lama also says, "If the situation or problem is such that is can be remedied, there is no reason to worry about it. Alternatively, if there is no way out, no solution, no possibility of resolution, then there is also no point in being worried about it, because you can't do anything about it anyway."[26] Simply put, if you are worrying and there's something you can do about the situation, then do something about it, and stop worrying. If you are worrying and there's nothing you can do about it, then there's no point in worrying because there's nothing you can do about it. Yes, it can be hard to put these ideas into practice, but if you can cultivate that mindset of living in the present, and if you can help cultivate in your child that mindset of living in the present, it can be highly effective in fighting the Worry Monster.

Of course, staying in the present is easier said than done. For example, last year doctors thought that my oldest daughter might have a serious medical condition. Part of the process of investigating the problem included my daughter seeing several specialists and having an eventual MRI. As you can imagine, the Worry Monster was spending a lot of time with me (at all hours of the day and night), telling me all of the awful things that could be diagnosed and all of the terrible future possibilities. I had to work very hard to stay focused in the present while reminding myself that we had several appointments scheduled and that we couldn't do anything more until we knew the facts. Fortunately, everything turned out fine. However, this serves as an example of how hard it was for me (an expert on banishing worry!) to try to stay in the present while acknowledging that there was nothing I could do about a potential problem that had yet to be discovered. And it also illustrates that I worried a lot over what turned out to be nothing.

> *I feel nervous on Sundays. I know the weekend is over, and I'm scared about going to school.*
>
> ~ nine-year-old warrior

Our goal—and I restate this goal at several points in this book, in several different ways—is to realize that all worrisome problems reside in the future, a time that has yet to exist. Thus, we can use our great thinking brains to solve any problem that occurs in the present, as opposed to worrying about every single problem before it actually happens in the future. Now you may counter my optimism by saying, "But there are patterns of behavior and experiences that let us know what's likely to happen." That may be true, but there is *still* nothing you can do about the situation *until* the birthday party tomorrow or *until* you have to take your child screaming from the car again to go to school. If these things are going happen, they are going to happen. You will have to deal with them when they do, and you *can* deal with them when they do.

Remember, you can put that worry in your handy dandy little worry box and pull it out another time (in the future). As a friend and colleague of mine said, "This helps because then I don't have to worry that I will forget to worry about it later." So should it ruin your night tonight? Should your child spend the entire week worrying about the music performance that doesn't happen until Friday? Worrying about a future event doesn't do anything except make us sleep-deprived, less patient, and more irritable. There is an old saying: "Don't trouble trouble 'til trouble troubles you."

Here is an example of what we are talking about. I had a meeting with a seventh grader and her mother to work on fighting the Worry Monster. The girl's worry centered around schoolwork, test performance, and her fears of getting in trouble, even though in reality she never got in trouble—it was simply something she worried *might* happen one day. The Worry Monster was holding strong, and I was running out of ideas of how to support this teen in letting go of her worries. I was reviewing all of her worries in my head when suddenly it hit me! *They were all future-based.* When I told her this, she didn't believe me because her worries seemed

so much in the present and right there in the room with us, like a bully breathing down her neck. I then listed them for her:

- ✔ "What if I do badly on the math test?"
- ✔ "What if I get caught talking in class?"
- ✔ "What if I don't make the soccer team?"
- ✔ "What if I don't get invited to the dance?"

As I continued to list them off, her eyes became as big as saucers. She sat quietly for some time. When she eventually spoke, she said, "Oh my gosh, it's true. None of them have happened yet!" I looked at her mother, who was sitting next to her. Her eyes were similarly wide open—like she was having her own "aha" moment. With a smile, she said, "I can't believe it. None of my own worries have happened yet either!"

So when your child is worrying, ask her what she is worrying about. It doesn't matter if she knows what the Worry Monster is telling her or not, or if she says, "I don't know why I'm feeling bad." Help her to focus on the present moment—right here, right now. It may take some practice to get the hang of this, but you will soon come to find that the present moment is almost always much better and more relaxed than the future worrisome one that hasn't yet occurred. Further, if we expand our awareness at the present moment, we may realize that the sun is shining, or we are sitting with someone who cares about us, or our favorite song may be on the radio, or nature around us is especially beautiful today, or something nice may have happened an hour ago. As Yogi Berra said, "The future ain't what it used to be!"

Letting Thoughts Pass

I want you to think about the image of King Kong on the top of a tall building swiping at fighter planes that are trying to destroy him. I often equate this image with the way we "Western thinkers" approach thinking: we often swat at and fight our thoughts. In addition, we often believe our own stinking thinking (which, of course, is what the Worry Monster wants us to do), even if the thinking is totally ridiculous and irrational.

Now I want you to visualize an airplane flying overhead pulling a banner that says, "Come join us at the county fair." You notice the plane and the banner as it is flying overhead, and then it is gone. About 10 minutes later, you notice the plane flying by again, and then again 10 minutes after that. Eventually, the plane with its banner is gone, back to its hangar, and you forget that the plane and its banner ever existed. This is a metaphor for noticing our thinking and then letting our thoughts pass as if they are inconsequential, like the banner advertising the county fair.

Mindfulness traditions suggest that our thoughts merely come to us, and who knows from where. So do we have to believe every irrational, worrisome, or scary thought the Worry Monster sends our way? No, we don't! We need to teach our children to notice their thoughts and then just let them pass without getting so attached to them or rattled by them. A mentor of mine once taught me to say, "Hmm…, interesting…," following an unpleasant thought. It's a surprisingly simple yet effective technique of distancing oneself from the content of the thought. The next time your child says, "I am afraid you will not come back to pick me up," have him say to himself, "Hmm…that's interesting because my mom always picks me up. She's never forgotten me once." He can even adopt a funny accent while saying this to further distance himself from the scary thought—to ridicule it.

Controlling Your Breathing

Breathing is free, and we can breathe as much as we want. The air is free. And breathing takes no effort, at least if we're healthy. Breathing is an automatic ability we are born with, and it is a necessary process required for living. Breathing is also something we take for granted. We don't always appreciate how our breathing can help us, but we can use breathing as a powerful tool for calming ourselves during times of stress, worry, and distress. We can focus on our breathing, slow it down, and feel more relaxed as it slows down. A yoga instructor once told me that regular, slow, deep breathing actually tricks our mind into feeling calm. Conscious breathing allows oxygen to flow through our body and brain and counteracts feelings of stress and anxiety.

Remember what happens when our survival response is triggered? When the amygdala gets involved? Blood leaves our brain to be utilized by our arms and legs. Deep breathing can keep our danger response from going off. It helps to keep blood in our brain and provides us with a feeling of relaxation.

> *My son developed an anxiety attack response to getting his blood pressure checked, which is something he had to do for his physicals for high school sports programs. I taught him how to focus on his breath while the cuff was on his arm, and it worked! He could get through having his blood pressure taken.*
>
> ~ father of a warrior

Activity: Belly Breathing

This is a very simple but important activity you can do by yourself and for yourself as you try to remain calm in the midst of daily parenting challenges; it is also something you can do with your child as part of her Worry Monster battle plan. Find a comfortable place where you and your child will not be interrupted. Lie down on your back, or sit on the floor yoga style, with your legs crossed in front of you. You can do the exercise sitting in a chair, too. It's something you can do anywhere—at home, at work, at school, in the car, in a meeting, at the end of the day to relax.

When you are ready to start, place your hands on your stomach or diaphragm. Keeping your hands on your stomach helps you check to make sure you are breathing deeply, not just through your chest, but through your belly. Belly breathing promotes relaxation, whereas breathing through your chest is associated with the survival response and running for your life (not relaxation!).

Take care to inhale slowly and then exhale slowly. You should feel your stomach muscles or diaphragm move up as you breathe in and down as you breathe out. Breathe through your nose, and be aware of the air moving in and out. Some yoga instructors suggest breathing in for the count of four seconds and then breathing out for the next four seconds. You can choose the number of seconds that feels comfortable for you. Some people like a four-count, others a six-count, while others prefer an eight-count. Again, do what feels right to you and your child.

Ready to practice? We are going to start with a six-count and do it six times. Put your hands on your stomach. Ready? Here we go.

Slowly inhale 1-2-3-4-5-6; now slowly exhale 1-2-3-4-5-6.
Again, slowly inhale 1-2-3-4-5-6; slowly exhale 1-2-3-4-5-6.
Slowly inhale 1-2-3-4-5-6; now slowly exhale 1-2-3-4-5-6.
Again, slowly inhale 1-2-3-4-5-6; slowly exhale 1-2-3-4-5-6.
Slowly inhale 1-2-3-4-5-6; slowly exhale 1-2-3-4-5-6.
And last time, slowly inhale 1-2-3-4-5-6,
and now slowly exhale 1-2-3-4-5-6.

Are you more relaxed now than you were merely a minute ago? I am guessing that your answer is yes because this technique almost *always* works, at least in the present moment. Remember, deep breathing tricks our brain into feeling relaxed. So if the Worry Monster tricks us into feeling scared, we can trick ourselves right back into feeling relaxed. Ha! Take that, Worry Monster!

It is important to practice breathing in calm times to be ready to use this powerful fighting strategy when the Worry Monster is messing with us. Make sure you don't expel more air than you breathe in because that alone can activate the anxiety response. People in the midst of a potentially anxiety-producing situation sometimes focus so much on breathing that they forget to exhale and then hyperventilate. That's when you breathe in more oxygen than is needed by your body.[27] You can feel sick from too much breathing in. The key is to breathe in slowly and breathe out slowly.

In order to practice slow and calm breathing, I highly recommend starting a regular family practice of breathing—one minute in the morning and one minute in the evening. Some families like to spend 5-15 minutes as they derive the positive effects of this simple practice of breathing and mindfulness. There is great benefit to quieting our minds and bodies and allowing room to breathe and just be. Like everything else, it takes practice. Since we are encouraging a team approach to fighting the Worry Monster, it is important for you to clearly model these techniques as something everyone should do, and not just your child who worries and is fearful. If your child sees you use techniques like deep breathing and staying in the present, she is more likely to buy into them and use them as well.

Things to Remember

✔ All worry exists in the future.

✔ Stay focused on the present moment.

✔ We don't have to believe our thoughts—let them pass.

✔ Deep breathing tricks our brain into thinking we are calm.

Things to Do

✔ Practice focusing on the present moment with your child. Only think about what is happening right now.

✔ Practice letting worrisome thoughts pass. Don't fight them; just notice them and say, "Hmm, it's interesting that I am thinking that thought."

✔ Practice deep belly breathing with your child for one minute initially; then increase the time as your child starts to feel comfortable with it and enjoys the relaxed feeling.

Chapter 8

Behavioral Interventions: Practice, Practice, Practice!

Act the way that you want to feel.

~ Gretchen Rubin

Now it's time to talk about the behavioral part of cognitive behavior therapy, often referred to as CBT. Behaviorism came to the fore in the 1950s,[28] countering the Freudian notion that people need to explore their unconscious mind and childhood history in order to make changes in their life. Behaviorism showed us that animals and people can learn to make behavioral changes by making systematic changes in their environment. Most of us don't like to think that we can be manipulated that easily by environmental reinforcements and changes, but alas, it's true. Thus, behaviorism became popular because people could make significant changes in their lives without years of psychoanalysis. In addition, as we discussed in Chapter 6 on cognitive interventions, it became clear that changing our behaviors changes our thinking and feelings, too, and so behavioral strategies complement cognitive strategies.

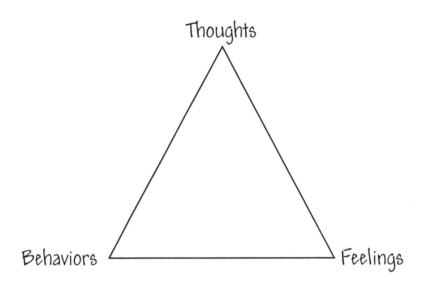

Behavioral strategies are particularly effective when you are working with a child who is young and/or is not ready for cognitive strategies that involve changing our thoughts. As we discussed earlier, some children and adolescents are not yet able to label their thinking. Additionally, their fear response may come so fast that they are not able to identify the thought that comes right before the awful physiological sensations caused by excessive adrenaline rushing through their bodies. These are the kids who keep telling you, "I don't know. I don't know what I'm thinking. *I told you, I don't know!*" They are so consumed with their feelings that they simply cannot talk about their thinking.

The wonderful thing about behavior strategies is that they can be developed by *doing* and by *practice*. Athletes, students, and musicians all use practice to build skills. Your child practices on the balance beam, practices free throws, practices tennis and golf, practices spelling and the times tables, practices driving, piano, guitar, and more. Why do we practice? We practice to get better at something. So how about practicing doing the things we're afraid of? Practice is the key to working through our fears. It is essential to practice behaviors that allow us to let go of the fears that are holding us back, preventing us from taking chances, and keeping us from meeting our potential and feeling good about ourselves.

There are a many effective behavior strategies that you can use with your child, along with the cognitive or thinking strategies we discussed earlier, to help him overcome the Worry Monster. You can also use behavioral strategies alone with children who are not ready to focus on their thinking. Here are some specific behavioral strategies:

- ✔ Systematic desensitization, success ladders, and baby steps
- ✔ Behavioral rehearsal
- ✔ Response inhibition
- ✔ Fake it to make it
- ✔ Pleasure predicting
- ✔ Taking a risk
- ✔ Prescribing failure

Systematic Desensitization, Success Ladders, and Baby Steps

Systematic desensitization is the fancy name for what actor Bill Murray called "baby steps" in the movie *What about Bob?* If you've seen the movie, you may recall that Bob overcame his fears by "putting one foot in front of the other." This strategy is also called a success ladder.[29] It involves breaking down an ultimate goal (let's say your child's goal is to go swimming) into small steps from least scary (looking at a picture of a pool or at a real pool from a distance) to most scary (putting her head under water). This technique is also called *exposure* because the person exposes herself to the thing she fears. The key principle involved in this intervention is that the person needs time to master each behavioral step, one at a time. Over time, by the end of the process, she becomes desensitized to the feared stimulus itself (she can go swimming without being afraid). This is a safe, gradual, and experimental approach to exposing a child to what she is afraid of.[30]

I would like to share a story about my daughter and how she faced her fear when she was in kindergarten and first grade. She had challenges at that age with separating from her mother and me and being in new situations by herself. It also took a long time for her to feel that a new situation wasn't new anymore—that is, the third month of school still felt like the first week of school to her, with a new teacher and a new classroom. Dropping her off at preschool was always a challenge because she wanted her mom or me to walk with her to the classroom, and while kindergarten was a bit easier than preschool, she still refused to walk into her kindergarten classroom by herself. She was very anxious about people looking at her, about who was going to be at the school drop-off, and about who knows what other scary things might happen. She absolutely refused to walk by herself from the parent drop-off zone into her school, and there was nothing we could say that would convince her. The school staff person who managed the car drop-off zone tried to bribe her with ice cream every day, but even though she loved ice cream, she still wouldn't leave the safety of the car and walk into her classroom by herself.

Realizing that most kids walk into school on their own in first grade, my wife and I started to practice with our daughter on walking into her class by herself during the second semester of her kindergarten year. At first I would walk her into her kindergarten classroom and follow her to her seat. Then, very slowly and over time, I would walk her only as far as the door and let her find her own seat. I would say, "How about I stand here?" "No! You have to come with me!" she would say. It was definitely a process, but we persisted.

Eventually, I would walk her only as far as her kindergarten cubby, which was just outside of her classroom door and enclosed in the fenced-in kindergarten area. Once she got used to that, I would walk her to the gate of the outside kindergarten area and let her walk to her cubby by herself. From there, we practiced walking to the corner of the building outside the kindergarten area, and that is far as we got by the end of kindergarten. It was not easy, as she really wanted me to walk with her all the way into her classroom most days.

Over the summer, my wife and I talked with her regularly about how one day soon I would drop her off in front of the school, and she would walk through the main school doors and into her first-grade classroom by herself. She was very fearful of doing this and continued to tell us, "No! I don't want to." At the end of summer, we went to the school site and practiced driving in the parking circle together a few times and then having her get out of the car and walk to the main entrance by herself. She could do this during the summer while the school was quiet and no one could see her, but would she do it when school actually started?

The first week of first grade, new first graders were given a week to get adjusted, so we carpooled to school taking other children. We drove her friend and then her cousin to school so that she could practice walking with one of them from the car into their classrooms. She did it! She got out of the car and walked into school, very fast and without me!

Finally, it was time—the deadline had arrived. It was the first day that first graders were supposed to walk into the school entirely by themselves. Just my luck, her cousin and friend wanted to be dropped off by their parents. So it was just her and me and the scary walk into school by herself. I talked with her during the drive to school about how she was "ready to do it," that it was "a piece of cake," and that I was proud of her for all of the practicing that she had done before the first day of school. We pulled in, drove around the corner, and there were all kinds of cars in front of and behind us, as well as a serious-looking person wearing an orange vest trying to keep things moving along.

My daughter was in her carseat looking around. "Things are looking good," I thought to myself. As we approached, I looked in the rearview mirror and saw her eyes get big, and she had a look on her face that said, "There is no way I am getting out of the car and walking into that school!" I said, "Look, we've been practicing; you can do this," and she said, "No, I'm not getting out. I'm not getting out. I'm not getting out!" Now even I was anxious, as the car line was moving and I was expected to keep it moving, yet I had a very stubborn and frightened little girl in my car who wouldn't get out. So like any good father of an anxious child, I said, "If you don't get out, I'm going to get in trouble with the principal!" It happened so fast that I wasn't exactly sure what I had said. To my surprise, she responded, "Fine!" And I'll never forget this: she grabbed her backpack, ripped off her seatbelt, opened the door, and walked into school by herself while I sat in the car sweating and panting.

When her mom picked her up after school, she said that our daughter walked out of school that day "about one foot taller" and with a great big smile on her face (not something she wore often at school). She even called several family members later that day to tell them what she had done.

My family's experience is both a story about taking baby steps toward an ultimate goal as well as an example meant to illustrate the importance of helping your child overcome worry in order to increase self-esteem and self-confidence.

Fast-forward four years—because this is also a story about how overcoming anxiety, one victory at a time over the Worry Monster, gradually adds up to changing your brain and your thinking in a more permanent way. When our daughter was a fifth grader, she had the nerve to make fun of her little first-grade sister for not wanting to walk into school on her own. She had totally forgotten how hard it had been for her to get out and walk in by herself at that same age. She actually said, "I can't even imagine why that would be scary." As I have found with many warriors, once a person gets over a fear or worry, she doesn't understand why she was afraid in the first place because the Worry Monster no longer has a hold on her.

As was the case with my daughter, practicing walking into school with "baby steps" toward a goal depended heavily on practicing small steps and not going too fast from A to Z. Many of us parents tend to be impatient with our kids and want them to go from A to Z quickly. We want our kids to "just do it!" Whatever they are afraid of may seem so silly to us and like it's wasting our time, as well as their own. We need to slow ourselves down and focus on helping them take small steps, not a big step, to get them to Step B.

Once they accomplish Step B over and over again, we can then get them to Step C. This is a process that ends at the finish line (Step Z), but it's like using the strategy of the tortoise in the fable about the tortoise and the hare.

It is important to prepare your child for each step by using expectant praise,[31] in which you praise the behavior that you want to see—for example, "It looks like you're getting ready to become a warrior against the Worry Monster. I admire how you seem to be thinking of the techniques we talked about and practiced!" Remind your child to focus on her breathing, to stay in the present, and to use positive self-talk. These techniques are often needed at each and every step to help her override her survival response and mount a victory.

Here is an example of systematic desensitization using a success ladder. Marcus is 10 and is very afraid of dogs. This fear has slowly but steadily grown and is affecting him and his family regularly. Marcus loves soccer, but he is afraid to go soccer practice and soccer games because there might be a dog there. His parents have gone through all of the cognitive techniques, but his fear response comes so quickly that he doesn't have time to talk himself through his fears. His response when he sees a dog is to escape and hide, and fast!

Marcus developed a success ladder with the help of his parents. The goal was to help him gradually expose himself to dogs with the ultimate goal of no longer being afraid of them. The ladder starts with the easiest step first and works its way up to the hardest and scariest steps. Another child with a fear of dogs might have a different set of steps, but the ladders all have the same basic setup. Here is Marcus's success ladder. The bottom rungs represent the easiest steps, and the top rungs indicate the goal to be achieved:

10+	Go to a public place with dogs that are allowed to play off leash.
10	Go to another friend's house with dogs.
9	Go to a friend's house with dogs roaming around.
8	Get close to a dog that is off leash.
7	Be far away from a dog that is off leash.
6	Pet a dog of choice that is on a leash.
5	See dogs more closely at an animal rescue or a dog park.
4	See dogs at a distance at an animal rescue or a dog park.
3	Be at a friend's house with a dog off leash outside or in another room.
2	Watch someone walking a dog on a leash.
1	Look at a book about dogs.

You will notice that Marcus's success ladder is numbered. These numbers represent SUDS (Subjective Units of Distress),[32] or what I call "scare ratings." When making a success ladder, it is important to have the child rate each worry or fear so that you and the child know where your starting point is (least scary) and what your ultimate goal is (most scary). Ask your child to give each situation or behavior a rating on a scale of 1 to 10 using the following scale:

✔ *1-3 Mild Discomfort*: Uncomfortable and apprehensive, butterflies, mild concern, palms are sweaty, knees feel weak

✔ *4-7 Moderate Discomfort*: Scared and anxious, more concern, dry mouth, wanting to leave or escape, feeling tense, trouble swallowing

✔ *8-10 Severe Discomfort*: Very scared and anxious (panic), headache, feeling trapped, dizzy, nauseous, numb, feeling like losing control

On Marcus's success ladder, he felt little distress when holding a book about dogs but was very afraid of being with dogs in an open public place. Being the conscientious person that he is, Marcus took his homework very seriously and practiced each rung, mounting victory after victory over the Worry Monster. I am happy to report that approximately one month after making his ladder, Marcus was able to participate in his soccer games without worry and fear, and he was able to go to parks where there were dogs off leash (and with a big smile on his face, too).

I suggest that you use a visual of a ladder, like Marcus's, to document your child's fear behaviors, and check them off as each victory occurs. This allows your child—and you—to see tangible progress, which helps increase motivation to keep going. One of my favorite parts of working with children to defeat their fears is seeing how great the kids feel when they finally tame the Worry Monster. I love the smiles on their faces when they are victorious!

I have another story that is powerful for all people who suffer from fear, and especially for folks who are afraid of insects. It is another example of systematic desensitization to overcome fear. I saw a video several years ago at a training seminar for CBT. It followed a woman through her journey to get over a phobia. First the video shows that the woman is so fearful of spiders that she almost faints when looking at a picture of a spider in a book from 15 feet or so away. Through systematic desensitization, baby steps, practicing breathing and relaxation, and getting used to the picture, she is able to take a step closer to the book, and then another step closer. She slowly is able to get closer to the picture, eventually to touch the picture, and then even to read the book. Then she does the same thing with a spider in a box, starting at the end of the room and moving closer and closer until she is sitting near the spider in the box, and then even holding the box. Finally, she does the same thing with a spider out of the box. Again she gets closer and closer, almost fainting from fear at times. At the end of the video she is holding a spider and laughing as the spider walks around on her hand. She did this for five hours over two days and was finally over her phobia!

Believe it or not, you can help your child do something very similar by using a success ladder and practicing each exposure over and over until it isn't scary anymore. It takes a ton of courage and a ton of support. That is why your child is lucky to have you on his team fighting the Worry Monster.

Activity: A Success Ladder for Parents
Think of a few things that you either avoid or are afraid of doing, and write them down on a piece of paper. Pick one behavior to focus on. Then:

✔ Break the behavior into 8-10 mini-steps (going from A to Z).

✔ Put a "scare rating" next to each behavior to quantify how uncomfortable or scary it is for you.

✔ List the behaviors in order from the least scary at the bottom to the most scary at the top in order to make a ladder.

✔ Start with the lowest rung on the ladder, and go for it. Do it a few times until it feels easy, and then go on to the next one.

What? You don't want to? Why not? Well, you may have just experienced what the Worry Monster does to your child. However, maybe you experienced a victory. If so, congratulations! This exercise is helpful for building empathy for what your child experiences as she thinks about and tries to take heroic steps against the Worry Monster. It's how victories can be won, one small step at a time.

Behavioral Rehearsal

Behavioral rehearsal is similar to systematic desensitization techniques in that "rehearsing" is doing the same feared thing over and over and over and over until it gets boring. You can't be bored and anxious at the same time. Anything that your child worries about can be done over and over again until he is bored with it and it no longer causes problems because it doesn't bring up anxious feelings anymore.

Like most of the strategies in this book, this is a simple task, yet it takes a lot of courage to do. If your child is afraid of heights or elevators, you will need to practice going up and down eleva-tors until it becomes boring. Remember, you can start by going up just one floor. If you're afraid of bridges, you go over bridges, over bridges, over bridges, and over more bridges. Dr. Liebgold, in his book *Freedom from Fear*, described conquering his own phobia of bridges; when he was ready to conquer that fear, he drove over every one of the seven Bay Area bridges every weekend and made at least two to four trips over a bridge daily until he no longer experienced any anxiety or fear.[33]

I have another story about my daughter. She had a lot of social anxiety and wouldn't look at people when they talked to her; she also wouldn't respond. She would freeze and stare off into the dis-tance. She wouldn't do this with family and close family friends, but she would with everyone else. So what do you do if your dad is a psychologist who can't stand the Worry Monster? You start practicing. First we practiced waving at people on our street when we drove by. Then we practiced saying hello to people on our street when we drove by with the window down. Before I knew it, she was practicing on her own, even when we weren't having a practice session. We then walked around our neighborhood and practiced saying hello to neighbors as we walked by them. It wasn't long before she was excited to answer our door (once she knew it wasn't a stranger) and say hi to whomever was on the other side. Just like walking her into school until she could do it on her own, I could see her confidence rise.

Fast-forward about two years to when she was a third grader and was invited to spend a day in her aunt's third-grade classroom. When the day was over, the other teachers told my sister-in-law that they were impressed with how my daughter had looked them all in the eye, shook their hand, and said, "Nice to meet you." We were blown away. How did that happen? Practice, practice, practice! If your child does the feared thing over and over, the fear will eventually go away. So pick a fear to work on with your child, and start practicing!

It is important to highlight the powerful avoidance response that inevitably shows up when we ask our child to do something she's afraid of. We often find ourselves debating, "Should I make her go to the party and endure the meltdown, or just let her skip it?" This is understandable, as a child's fear response, as you well know, can be severe and intense. However, you now know how important it is to help your child take a step against the Worry Monster. So take some deep breaths and get ready to help her manage the worry and fear. Maybe you need to start smaller, or perhaps this is just something that she needs to be strongly encouraged to do. Just like the story of my daughter finally walking into school by herself, she was stronger than she thought and had the tools to handle the situation. And I learned that *I* could handle the situation in the face of the Worry Monster working on both of us. I think you will learn that your child (and you) can handle the Worry Monster better than you may think.

> *When I first started piano lessons, I didn't know how to read music, so I tried to memorize everything so no one would know. After a while that got harder to do. At home when I was practicing, I would get frustrated and start to cry. Sometimes I would even get up from the piano and walk away. I thought I would get it eventually, but I didn't. I was so afraid that my teacher would be angry and disappointed in me. My mom finally made me tell my teacher that I couldn't read music. I was very worried, but she wasn't mad! We kept practicing, and suddenly, snap! I got it! I still can't read all of the notes, but I am getting better, and I'm not scared of not knowing anymore.*
>
> ~ nine-year-old warrior

Response Inhibition

Response inhibition is used primarily for helping people with Obsessive-Compulsive Disorder. Remember that a core feature of OCD is doing a compulsive or repetitive behavior (i.e., turning the light switch off and on repeatedly) in order to release tension and anxiety around a repetitive, irrational, and anxious thought (such as worrying that something bad might happen). A child with OCD or with OCD behaviors knows that the thoughts the Worry Monster are telling him are irrational and are likely never going to happen, yet he is not willing to take the chance. Further, the anxiety and tension are so uncomfortable that there is a very strong need to make them go away by doing the behavior.

The problem is that engaging in a compulsive behavior reinforces and solidifies the belief that the irrational thought is something to be afraid of and obeyed and that the compulsive behavior is the only thing that can make the feared thought and bad feelings go away. So the response inhibition technique is exactly what it sounds like: the goal is for your child to inhibit or stop his response to what the Worry Monster (whom we can now call the OCD Monster) is telling him.

Here are some examples of behaviors that might focus on inhibiting a compulsion: resisting or reducing hand-washing, resisting touching things a particular number of times, resisting repeating what somebody says, resisting walking a certain way down the hall, resisting washing in the shower in a precise order, and so on. One effective way to help increase the response inhibition is by using a timer. The goal is to see how long the child can keep from doing the behavior. Start small, maybe initially setting the timer for only three minutes, but working up to longer and longer times. It helps to distract your child during this time so that he's not mentally focusing on the stinking thinking thoughts. Before long, your child will see that he can hold off doing the behavior. You may want to help your child make a chart of how long he's able to go without doing the behavior so that he can see how he's improving. This allows him to realize that he has some control over his behavior and that he can withstand the uncomfortable feelings. Further, it allows him to see that the irrational thought the OCD Monster is telling him is not true—the scary thing the monster tells him will happen if he doesn't do the behavior doesn't actually happen.

Another way to battle the OCD Monster is to have your child try to stop doing something so many times if he feels like he needs to repeat a behavior to feel okay. For example, maybe your child feels like he has to touch the doorway on both sides five times each before he can go into his room. But instead of doing that, you ask him to see if he can touch the doorway only four times. And when that becomes easy, he can decide to touch the doorway only three times. Eventually, he will learn that he doesn't need to do it at all, and then he'll know that he's conquered that monster! You can keep a chart to track this kind of progress, too. Just have your child write down how many times he did the behavior each day, and he'll be able to see that he's the one who's in control of what he does—not the monsters!

Fake It to Make It

This is another good strategy for managing our brain and tricking the Worry Monster. Your child might be scared, but she also may be good at drama, both in and out of formal performances. The goal of "fake it to make it" is to help her put on an Academy Award-winning performance. So you say to your child: "I want you to pretend that you are going to have fun. Just pretend. Fake it. I'll give you a reward if you can fake it. If you can make me think that you are having fun or that you are not afraid, we can go and get that (toy, book, magazine, smoothie) you wanted."

We will be talking about reinforcement and motivation techniques later, but as a foreshadowing, incentivizing is very important for helping a child do something that she does not want to do, and even more so if she is afraid of doing it.

Now back to faking it. If a child can fake a behavior or an experience, it changes her neurochemistry, and it actually changes her feelings. For example, research has shown that planned smiling and laughing changes our mood in a positive way.[34] When your child is smiling, it's impossible for her to be as upset as she is when she is crying. You can help your child trick the Worry Monster (and herself) into having fun and being less worried and scared.

No matter how much Will studied, he worried that he was not prepared for his test and was going to do poorly. I challenged him to pretend that he was prepared and to tell himself over and over, "I am prepared; I am always prepared." Will was convinced it wouldn't work; however, he agreed to try. He was pleased to find out that it helped him to feel more confident and to focus on the test.

~ mother of a warrior

Fumiko does not like to be away from her father and me.
Although she loves gymnastics, she's afraid to go the class.
So I promised her that we would get a frozen yogurt if
she could trick her instructor by walking in with a smile,
saying hi to him, and walking onto the mat (unlike every
other day). We laughed at how funny it would be to see
her teacher shocked at her behavior. I know she'll still be
nervous, but Fumiko is willing to try it.

~ mother of a warrior

I once had a client who became nervous in many situations, and finally he became frustrated with feeling that way. He decided that he was going to" act like a winner." When in social situations, he would ask himself, "What would a winner do?" He was surprised at how he was able to feel and act confident when he simply pretended to be a winner. Over time, he admitted that he found himself acting like a winner without giving it much thought. To summarize this point concisely and to help your child remember it, you can say it this way: *Act the way you want to feel.*

Faking it may seem artificial, especially at first. I have had children tell me, "But it's not really me. I'm just pretending." This is a legitimate statement. So I tell them that I understand what they are saying, but we are just going to keep trying the behavior as an experiment to see what happens. The thing is, after doing it for awhile, they begin to incorporate the new behavior into who they are and forget that they questioned it in the first place.

Pleasure Predicting

Pleasure predicting is similar and complementary to the "fake it to make it" technique. Many children have anticipatory anxiety, meaning they get really worked up over something that has yet to occur, like a party, performance, or dance, but then once they are at the actual event, they are fine. The act of getting your child to an event when he experiences anxiety about it is quite a task; it's like pulling teeth every time. That's because the Worry Monster is telling your child something that is making him nervous. He may be worried about all of the things that *could* go wrong and that he is sure *will* go wrong.

Pleasure predicting can help your child learn more about himself and help him find a way to fight the Worry Monster. Here is how it works. You say to your child, "Okay, on a scale of 1-10, how awful is it going to be when you're there? 10 is great, and 1 is awful. 1? Okay, let's see how it goes and if you were right about how bad it will be."

Sometimes your child will simply be willing to go to show you that he was right and that it really was awful. However, my experience is that it often is not as bad as he thinks it's going to be. After the event you may say, "So how was it? A 5? That's not too bad. I guess it was a little better than you thought."

Remember that you don't want to make this about your child being wrong. You need to talk to him about it in a way that allows him to be open to admitting that it was better than he thought. Over time, this helps him to see his patterns of thinking, and we want to help him increase his self-knowledge. Self-knowledge is power. If he learns that he tends to always think that things are going to be a 1 but that things usually end up being a 5 or a 7, then he will begin to internalize that the Worry Monster tries to make him think that things are going to be worse than they ultimately are.

When reviewing the event with your child, ask him what went well and what didn't. The goal is to try to learn more about how the Worry Monster affects him, as well as to help him gain more insight about the Worry Monster and to develop tools to conquer him. Do not be surprised, however, if your child does not want to talk about his successes. Children often do not want you to think that they are fine and not nervous anymore. If your child doesn't want to discuss it, don't make it a big deal. It may be the only way he is willing to take steps against the Worry Monster at first—by just doing the behavior. Success can build this way, as this is the basis of behavior interventions.

> *I moved to a new school and was scared to buy lunch. I was afraid that I might not like what they were serving.*

One day one of my new friends said, "The lunch today is really good." And I just decided, that's it. I am going to do it. And I did—and it really was good! Now I am not afraid to buy lunch, and I've even tried new foods that I never thought I'd like before.

~ nine-year-old warrior

Taking a Risk

Planned risk taking is a great technique for worriers and perfectionists. Perfectionists are really good at only doing things they think they can do well, like only turning in schoolwork that is "perfect." So an anti-perfectionistic strategy is to challenge your child to take a risk at something that she's not good at, to try something new, and to turn something in that is just okay but not perfect. This is something that we have to model for kids all the time and talk about at the dinner table, at the breakfast table, and in the car. Talk about something you tried at work, about a joke you told that nobody understood, about when someone laughed at you, about how you put the thing in the wrong box, how you had food in your teeth and didn't know it, and so on.

Our children model themselves after us. If we want them to do something new or something they don't think they are great at, we need to model it for them and then challenge them to do the same. You can even make this a family challenge: ask everyone to do one scary thing for the week, and then report back at dinner on Sunday. Another fun twist is to have a contest, and the person who has the worst experience, as voted by the family, wins a prize.

My parents and even my teacher kept telling me to just turn in my project—that it was more than fine the way it was. They kept saying that it didn't matter that much for my grade and that it was "good enough." I wasn't happy with it and kept finding things that could be done better. Finally, I was exhausted and sick of working on it, so I just made myself turn it in. It felt good to be done with it. I did fine on it and realized that I wasted a lot of time trying to make it perfect when it just needed to be good.

~ 16-year-old warrior

Prescribing Failure

Prescribing failure is similar to taking a risk, as it challenges perfectionists to do something that is not perfect and to survive it. You may think that *survive* is too dramatic a word, but it's really what a perfectionist feels—that he won't be able to survive or go on if something does not come out just right. This type of thinking is restrictive, debilitating, and often quite painful. So ask your artist to turn in an art piece that is not "just right." Or, better yet, tell your perfectionistic student not to study for a quiz. Now you might be thinking, "What are you talking about?!" But think about it this way: we want children who worry too much to learn to worry less. On the flip side, we want children who don't worry about much to "worry" or think a little more. However, you are not reading this book because you have a child who doesn't worry enough. You have a child who is likely worrying too much—or at least more than you would like. Your child is probably a highly conscientious person who wants to do really well and who spends a lot of energy thinking about it, and maybe doing it, too. Challenge your child to do something less than perfect, and let him experience that he is still loved and that the world will not crash in on him for it. This is a way to show him that what the Worry Monster is telling him about needing to be perfect is simply not true. You will still love him, even when he turns in work that is not perfect.

> *I am quite the perfectionist and want everything to be perfect. Thursday nights are the worst for me. People say that once you get past Wednesday, the week gets easier. Nope, not true. Thursday nights are my meltdown nights. Thursday nights are the nights during which I somehow manage to conjure up every possible thing that I could need to worry about; the most trivial thing becomes magnified*

*so it is of just as much importance as the biggest thing.
I'm typically told just to go to bed and everything thing
will be better in the morning, and it always is. My mom
tells me that she actually wants me to fail, as in get an F
on something. She's not a bad mom; she just wants me to
have that experience of not getting everything perfect or
close to perfect.*

> ~ 15-year-old warrior

I had a client recently whose school came up with a wonderful
activity to help their students take risks and embrace failure. They
went on a fieldtrip to a local mall, where the assignment was to
get rejected for employment from 10 different stores. My 15-year-
old client, who had significant anxiety, came into an appointment
with me beaming and stating that he had won the grand prize.
His confidence grew so much with each rejection (because he was
supposed to get rejected) that he decided to apply to be a manager
at a Victoria's Secret store. He laughed as he described the faces of
the people who worked there and the customers who were in line.
He said, "I never knew how fun it could be to be rejected!"

Some examples of other ways to challenge your perfectionist
to make mistakes include having him ask friends over to play when
you know they are going to be busy, having him try to be last in a
contest at school, or telling him to spill milk on his clothes at lunch.
It actually can be fun to have a brainstorming session with your
child in which you both come up with the funniest ways you can
think of to make a mistake or to fail. You can even each pick one
for the other to do. Remember, kids love knowing that they are not
alone in this, and they are motivated by the knowledge that you are
fighting the Worry Monster, too.

More Interventions for Perfectionism

*Sometimes (okay, maybe not just sometimes) I will see
that someone is a better dancer, writer, etc. than me,
and I'll want to give up. Sometimes I avoid seeing that*

imperfection/inferiority in myself by not letting myself be second best, pushing myself to be the best at everything. I can accept that I'm not the best at something if it is something that is new to me, but if I know I can do it and know I am good at it, it is hard to swallow the fact that I am not the best.

~ 14-year-old warrior

Sticking to the Plan

As you may know from your little perfectionist at home, procrastination is a common problem. Perfectionists often feel intimidated by even simple projects because they are daunted by the idea that they need to make them perfect. Besides, it's easier to blame a lack of perfection on the fact that a project wasn't finished rather than because it's simply impossible to be perfect all the time. If a project is finished but not perfect, that "proves" their ineptitude, but if a project isn't perfect because it's not finished, that's just circumstance.

An effective anti-procrastination technique is to help your child choose a topic or activity of focus, make a plan to accomplish the task, and then actually stick to the plan. This is not as easy as it sounds, since perfectionists often find new or "better" ways to do something or feel that they need to learn or do more than the task requires. I once had a client who turned every writing assignment into a Master's thesis. Needless to say, this very bright person wasn't able to keep up with her work and fell further and further behind.

There is an old saying: *The perfect is the enemy of the good.* This means that when we try too hard for perfection, we often end up not performing or not turning in something that is good or "good enough"—which is usually all we need to do.

It is important for parents to check in with their own perfectionistic tendencies, too. I have found that I have to put my own expectations and ideas aside when trying to help my child be less of a perfectionist. Remember, when a perfectionist turns in less-than-perfect work or decides that the work is "good enough," that is a *good* thing. The last thing we want to do is point out how an assignment could be done a little better. Easy to say, but hard to do.

> *Sometimes when people tell me "Good job!" I only half believe them because in the back of my mind, I'm thinking about all of the other things that I could have done and all of the little mistakes I made.*
>
> ~ 15-year-old warrior

Setting Realistic Expectations

Setting realistic expectations can also be helpful for combating perfectionism.[35] Before your child starts a task, signs up to be in a play, or joins a team, discuss what expectations she has for herself. Listen closely, and see whether you think the expectations are reasonable or leave little room for anything but being the best. Remind her that she doesn't have to do everything right the first time. Try to help her come up with "good enough" expectations that she can shoot for so that you can help remind her of them when she gets stuck.

It is important that you and your child agree on the plan and that the plan is realistic. Remember, many parents have perfectionistic tendencies, too, and our kids know this about us. Therefore, it is important for your child to know that you truly will be okay with her not being the best and not turning in exceptional or "perfect" work. Sometimes it helps to make a written plan, actually writing down the agreed-upon guidelines for the assignment, activity, or event. This makes the goal concrete. And it can be simple, such as writing down the actual instructions for a school assignment as such: "Write two sentences for each question," when your child usually writes a page for each.

> *A lot of the time I'm worried when I get time reminders during in-class writings and tests because I'm not sure that I will have enough time to write down everything I want to say.*
>
> ~ 15-year-old warrior

It can also be liberating for a child to join a sports team or an activity with the goal of just having fun. Perfectionists are so focused on being the best that fun often does not come into the picture. It is a gift for a perfectionist to participate in something and not have to always be "on." Maybe your written goal will be this: "Do NOT win the race." This gives your child permission to not be the best and yet to realize that the world still turns, the sun still comes up, her friends still like her, and you still love her. The Worry Monster (or his good friend the Perfectionist Monster) often tells your child (and maybe you) that the aforementioned bad things will happen. He is lying, but he is very convincing, as we well know.

Planning Alternative Paths

Planning positive alternative paths is another useful strategy for perfectionist thinkers. Most perfectionists believe that there is only one way to do something: the best! This is usually not because they have a superiority complex; it is because they feel that they have failed if they produce anything less than that. It is important to help your child develop more flexible and less rigid thinking. Talk with him about there being more than one solution to many problems. Help him to tolerate and eventually embrace uncertainty. As mentioned previously, give him permission to make mistakes. Finally, help him come up with several possibilities and options.

> *Devin, age 12, always comes up with elaborate ideas for her projects. If the assignment is to write a paper about an influential person, Devin writes about three people who started a movement. If the assignment is to sketch a nature scene, Devin sketches and then paints it in watercolor. While the product is often impressive, the process is grueling for her, and also for her parents. Devin is very hard on herself, often feeling that her work is not good enough. She comes into her parents' room regularly late at night crying and upset, saying she can't do it, and they don't understand her.*

Devin's parents have decided that they need to help their daughter come up with a contingency plan for her next project—a five-page research paper on an almost extinct species. So they begin by asking her what she is going to research and help her determine the amount of time she needs to complete the project. They then agree on bedtime (since she often stays up late) and what she is willing to turn in if she runs out of time. They also tell her what they are willing to support (answering questions and sitting with her prior to 9:00 in the evenings) and what they are not willing to support (late-night meltdowns). They tell her that their goal for her is to turn in a project on time that is "good enough." They know that there will be challenges along the way, but they are committed to helping her develop coping skills.

Does Devin sound familiar to you? This story is very common. Late-night meltdowns and accusations to parents who "don't understand" are unfortunate facts of life in many homes of perfectionistic students. Perfectionists need to know that "many roads lead to

Rome," not just one. Help your child develop alternate paths and contingency plans. Plan ahead to help thwart the expected challenges that the Worry Monster will set up. Remember, while the Worry Monster is sneaky, he is also predictable.

Increasing Motivation and Reducing Stress

Reinforcement

It's time to talk about motivating and incentivizing. Some people think that incentivizing is the same as bribing. I think it is different; the word *bribe* holds a negative connotation, as though you're trying to get someone to do something bad or even illegal. Terms like *motivating, incentivizing, reinforcing*, and *rewarding* are better words that more accurately depict the positive direction we want to encourage our children to go in. And let's be honest: the adult world works through an incentivizing system. How many salespeople would make 100 cold calls a day if they would get paid the exact same amount for making only 10 calls? Exactly! Very few would, since most people are motivated by more money, more time, more flexibility, etc. Incentive plans are made to help a person engage in a desired behavior (usually for the benefit of the company) by offering rewards.

Okay, so how many adults do you think would choose to conquer their worst fear just for fun? I think you know where I'm going with this. I have rarely seen a child choose to work on his fear and worry unless he is very motivated to do so for a reason that is important to him—an intrinsic or personal reason. This does happen, but often it is when a child very much desires, for example, to have a sleepover, to go on the school overnight trip at the zoo, or to visit a place that requires going over a bridge. Most children need some motivation—some incentive—to tackle a fear. Remember, the natural response is usually to avoid the fear.

There are two basic ways to motivate your child. One is by *adding* a reward, and the other is by *removing* or *taking away* something. The first way is through positive reinforcement (adding a reward), and the other is through negative reinforcement (removing something or eliminating a task or chore that the child doesn't like to do). But in both cases you are reinforcing a desired behavior, meaning you are increasing the likelihood of the behavior occurring again in the future. And in both cases, the reinforcement is *desired* by the child. For example, your child may get 15 minutes of screen time for engaging in a practice session of looking at people when talking to them, or he may not have to rake the leaves for going up and down the elevator three times. Remember, it is important to reward steps toward the goal, not just the goal itself. We want to set up opportunities for the child to have success and victories against the Worry Monster.

It is important when incentivizing not to make threats ("If you don't, then…") or to punish a child for fearful behavior and/or not trying a baby step. Not only does this usually not work, it increases a child's fear response and reduces his ability to use his thinking brain to overpower his survival response. Further, we ultimately want the process of taming the Worry Monster to be positive and not one that is dreaded and feared.

Reducing External Stressors

It is very important that we don't inadvertently reinforce our child's avoidance behavior by doing things for her that she needs to learn to do herself—for example, ordering her food for her at a restaurant so that she doesn't have to talk to and make eye contact with the waiter. The more we do this, the more we are teaching her to feel helpless and to succumb to the Worry Monster. What we want is for her to be independent and self-sufficient. That said, wherever possible, it is important to take efforts to decrease the level of external stress by making modifications in the environment. One good way to do this is to have an "emergency plan" to help reduce anxiety. It helps for a child to know what do to when she feels nervous or scared.

For example, if your child gets nervous at school or worries about having an anxiety attack, identify a "go to" person at the school whom she can talk to in order to help calm herself down. If the child has reading challenges, attention challenges, or intense social anxiety, ask her teacher not to call on her to read out loud (at least not without a plan). If the child is nervous about tests, work with her teacher to find some ways to reduce her test anxiety, like taking the test in a quiet environment or allowing the child more time so she doesn't worry as much about not finishing. Another option is to take the test early before school starts so the child doesn't have to worry about it all day. The goal is to slowly take steps against the Worry Monster so that these accommodations are eventually not needed. Simply put, it is often necessary to temporarily reduce some of the environmental stress on your child so that she can take successful steps against the Worry Monster. You want to make sure that you are modifying the environment while you are helping your child gain victories over the Worry Monster, but you don't want to prevent your child from doing things she is already comfortable doing.

Promoting Resilience

Remember when I mentioned in the introduction that this book could also be called *A Parent's Toolbox for Raising Resilient Kids*? Guess what? You now have learned the essential ingredients for raising a resilient child! Leading resiliency researchers and practitioners Karen Reivich and Andrew Shatté talk about four key resilience skills for children and adolescents that may sound familiar to you. These are the skills:[36]

- ✔ *ABCs*: In order to respond to adversity (the "A"), people must recognize their beliefs (the "B") in their thoughts and then engage in challenging those thoughts (the "C"). In this way, they can learn the connection between their thoughts, feelings, and behaviors. They need to learn to ask themselves questions about what they are thinking and how they can think differently.

- ✔ *Challenge Beliefs*: Teach kids to notice their thinking style and to generate alternatives. Teach them to look for evidence to determine whether their thinking is accurate.

✔ *Putting It in Perspective*: Practice preparing for a challenging situation in the future. Generate worst-case beliefs and then healthier, more realistic counter-beliefs, and then make a plan for dealing with the situation.

✔ *Real-Time Resilience*: Have a plan that consists of the other three skills to manage adversity when it arises.

So there you have it. By teaching kids about how to tame the Worry Monster—understanding how their survival response works, learning that their thoughts determine their emotions and behaviors, understanding that changing their thinking changes their feelings, and learning that practicing doing scary behaviors makes them stronger—they will have the necessary skills to take on all of life's adversities and become resilient!

Things to Remember

✔ Changing behaviors changes thoughts and feelings.

✔ Worries and fears can be broken down into baby steps.

✔ Doing a small feared or worrisome behavior is an important step against the Worry Monster.

✔ Practicing the feared behavior over and over makes the Worry Monster go away.

✔ Not doing what the Worry Monster (OCD Monster) tells you to do makes the monster weaker.

✔ Pretending to not be scared helps a person do a scary thing (and maybe even enjoy doing it).

✔ It is a victory when a perfectionist can be okay with "good enough" work and effort.

✔ Children need motivators or reinforcers to engage in behaviors that are scary to them.

✔ Teaching children these skills is teaching them to be resilient and preparing them for life.

Things to Do

- ✔ With your child, choose a scary or worrisome behavior or activity, and break the behavior into 8-10 mini-steps.

- ✔ Teach your child about "scare ratings," and put a rating next to each behavior to quantify how uncomfortable or scary it is for him.

- ✔ List the behaviors in the form of a success ladder, with the least scary at the bottom and the most scary at the top.

- ✔ Set up a reinforcement plan so that your child is motivated to do the scary behavior.

- ✔ Start with the first behavior on the list, and have your child practice doing it.

- ✔ Have your child do the behavior a few times until it feels easy, and then go on to the next one.

- ✔ Repeat the process until your child has conquered the fear.

CHAPTER 9

Patrick, Savannah, and Drew

*Don't believe everything you think. Thoughts are just that—
thoughts.*

~ Allan Lokos

I would like to introduce you to Patrick, Savannah, and Drew, three
courageous young people I know. They know the Worry Monster
well, and so do their parents. They have graciously given permission to use their stories so that others can learn to fight the Worry
Monster as they have. Through their experiences, you will see how
understanding the fear response in their bodies, becoming aware
of the Worry Monster and his tricks and tactics, and developing
thinking and behavior plans helped them regain control of their
lives and drive the Worry Monster away. (Their names have been
changed to protect their privacy.)

Patrick

Patrick is a 10-year-old fifth grader. His parents say that he's a
sweet and sensitive boy who "feels a lot of things." He is talkative,
engaging, loves people, and is a "pleaser," as he always wants to do
the right thing and make others happy. Patrick's family moved to
another state when he was three. That was a difficult transition for

him, and he began having problems sleeping. His parents reported that he started showing other signs of anxiety during the week before kindergarten, when his older sister was diagnosed with diabetes, a serious medical condition. Patrick started to worry that his mother was going to die. He became tense and insecure, and he didn't want to leave his mother's side. He started to cry more than usual and became easily upset in situations that normally were not a problem for him.

Despite these difficulties, kindergarten through fourth grade went relatively well for Patrick. Schoolwork was easy for him, with the exception of reading. He had some difficulty decoding words and reading fluently, but he received helpful tutoring. In fifth grade, however, Patrick began fretting over even minor issues, and he started washing his hands several times a day. His parents recall that he had done this off and on in first grade as well. These behaviors were most likely brought on by a new and worrisome issue at home: due to changes in the economy, Patrick's father's job was in jeopardy, and there was discussion of the family selling their home and moving out of state. Patrick's parents described how their son began a process of jumping in and out of bed several times at bedtime, and they noticed that he touched certain objects and people over and over and also tapped himself in a particular way. He had trouble sleeping and often had bad dreams.

Patrick admitted to jumping out of bed when he was tired, jumping up and touching the tops of doorways, washing his hands a lot, and switching the light switch on and off "to get rid of the freaky feelings." He also "needed" to touch somebody, "needed" to touch part of his body ("to balance it"), and "needed" to touch someone again if it didn't feel right the first time. Patrick said that he felt angry and scared that something bad would happen if he didn't do those things. His worst times were when he had to transition to another task or activity, when there was an unexpected change, or at the thought of something changing.

What Neighborhood Is Patrick In?

What is going on for Patrick? Let's run through some questions and answers to see if we can come to a clearer understanding of what we can do to help him. Thinking about these questions in the context of how they can be answered for Patrick's situation will help you answer the same questions for your child.

Q: What are Patrick's primary symptoms?
A: Worrying, washing hands, touching people and objects, trouble sleeping, nightmares

Q: What are some of his primary stressors?
A: Moving, new school, sister diagnosed with diabetes, dad's changing job, possible move

Q: What possible anxiety neighborhoods is he in?
A: Worry, OCD

Q: What strategies can be used to help him?
A: Teach him about our fight or flight response; help him learn about the Worry and OCD Monsters and what they say to him; work on response inhibition to help him resist doing the things he thinks he "needs" to do; challenge and change his thinking; teach him about worry time, and make a worry box

Helping Patrick Fight the Worry and OCD Monsters

Helping a child develop strategies and gain tools to fight the Worry Monster is a creative endeavor that takes thought and persistence. It involves understanding how the Worry Monster works for each individual. As you will see, in order to give Patrick the tools he needed to fight the Worry Monster, we had to use several techniques and strategies.

The first thing we did was to help Patrick understand the fight or flight response. We externalized the problem by developing language that placed the problem outside of him, naming two monsters and calling them the Worry Monster and the OCD Monster. We developed a detailed understanding of how the monsters become tricky and powerful. We then developed strategies to undermine the Worry and OCD Monsters' power, and we put together a team, led by his father and supported by his mother, to conquer the two monsters. Finally, we developed a "toolbox" of strategies that Patrick could carry with him at all times.

What follows are a few examples of how to talk about the Worry and OCD Monsters with your child. By asking simple questions, I was able to help Patrick learn quite a bit about his monsters and gain a sense of control over them. You can ask your child the same kinds of simple questions.

Identifying Patrick's Irrational and Worrisome Thoughts

Dan: "What does the OCD Monster say to you?"

Patrick: "The OCD Monster always says something bad is going to happen. He makes me feel that I have to touch things and wash my hands or something bad will happen."

Changing Patrick's Thinking

Dan: "How can you change your thinking? What can you tell the Worry and OCD Monsters so they don't trick you?"

Patrick started to talk back to the monsters. Whenever he would think the scary thoughts, he would respond by saying to himself: "The monster doesn't have magic powers. My team is stronger and more powerful than he is. He's just a bully and a coward."

Patrick's Success Ladder and Scare Steps

Once Patrick knew about the fight or flight response, and that the Worry and OCD Monsters tell him things to make him worried and scared, and that he could change his thinking to have more rational and less scary thoughts, we created a success ladder for him, with 1 being the easiest step and 10 being the hardest at the top rung of the ladder. The numbers on the left represent his scare ratings. You'll notice that Patrick's ladder is not filled with things he must do, but instead it consists mostly of things that he must try *not* to do.

10	Touching something he has been afraid of
9	Resist touching another person
7-8	Resist jumping in and out of bed
5-6	Resist touching various parts of his body
4	Resist washing hands
3	Resist turning light switches on and off
1-2	Resist touching doorways

Response Inhibition

Patrick started with the least scary behavior on his list, and each week he practiced not doing the behavior the OCD and Worry Monsters told him he had to do. He worked on a behavior until it became a 1 and then moved on to the next rung on the ladder.

Touching doorways and turning light switches on and off quickly became a 1.

Patrick developed a healthier ritual of washing his hands just three times a day instead of six or seven times. Eventually this new habit became a 1.

Patrick continued to work his way up the ladder. Some days were tougher than others, but with the support of his parents, he kept practicing. As he experienced victories over the Worry and OCD Monsters, he became more and more motivated to continue to battle them.

However, Patrick's worry continued. Even though Patrick achieved victory after victory over the OCD Monster, the Worry Monster not only remained, but at times became stronger. Now Patrick started to worry about natural and other disasters happening—tsunamis, plane crashes, tornados, and floods. Losing ground like this is common when fighting worry and anxiety, as the Worry Monster is stubborn and does not like to lose his power. Be assured that this is part of the process and merely requires continued persistence, practice, and perseverance. In addition to continuing to challenge and change Patrick's thinking, we developed more strategies for fighting the Worry Monster.

Strategies for Combating Worry

✔ *Schedule worry time*: Patrick decided that he would set aside 15 minutes in the evening to worry. So when he was worrying during the day, he would tell himself, "I will save this for my worry time later tonight." He found that this helped distract him from his worry throughout the day, and he often forgot what his worry had been about when night came.

✔ *Make a worry box*: As many children I know have experienced, Patrick loved the idea of making and decorating a worry box. He would write down his worries in the morning and at night (when he could remember them) and place them in his worry box for safe-keeping. That meant that the worries were in the box and away from him, creating space between him and the worries.

Coping Plan: Toolbox

We developed a "toolbox" that Patrick could take with him wherever he went, and he could use it whenever the OCD or Worry Monster came for a visit. While Patrick kept his toolbox in his head, some kids like to keep theirs on a small notepad or a note card they carry with them in their pocket or backpack. With these tools, Patrick felt more prepared and equipped to fight the monsters whenever they showed up. His toolbox consisted of these strategies:

✔ Breathe calmly.

✔ Visualize a calming place.

✔ Know your triggers.

✔ Identify your thoughts: *How are my thoughts making me worry?*

✔ Challenge the thoughts, change the thoughts, and talk back to the Worry Monster and the OCD Monster.

✔ Motivate yourself to face the fear, and give yourself a reward.

✔ Remind yourself that anxious feelings *always* go away eventually.

✔ Practice doing the positive behaviors over and over.

✔ *Refuse* to let worry and anxiety run your life!

Patrick's Success Ladder After Scaring Away the Worry Monster
Was Patrick successful? I think so. Here is how he now rates these behaviors:

✔ Not touching doorways: 0
✔ Not turning light switches on and off: 0
✔ Not washing hands: 3
✔ Not touching himself: 0
✔ Not jumping in and out of bed: 0
✔ Not touching someone: 0
✔ Touching something scary: 0

Patrick's Current Thinking

✔ "The OCD Monster uses fiction just like in my books."

✔ "Science calms me. I am going to learn more about natural disasters."

✔ "I don't let the OCD Monster bully me like I used to."

✔ "I just tell myself that he can't do the things he says he will do."

✔ "When I live with it, it goes away; when I fight it, it makes me do it over and over again."

Patrick's Worry and OCD Monsters come back to visit from time to time, particularly when there is a new, big transition like a move or a new school. However, Patrick knows his monsters well and uses his toolbox to deal with them. His parents remind him of how to challenge his thinking and about all of the successes he's had. As a result, the OCD and Worry Monsters do not hang around much anymore, and they certainly are less powerful than they used to be.

Savannah

Savannah is an 11-year-old sixth grader. She is a very bright child who, according to her parents, has always been "intensely emotional, observant of her surroundings, and sensitive." Savannah is very perceptive, has an excellent memory, and has always done very well in school. She saw a school counselor in third grade to help her deal with relationship challenges, as she was more emotional than usual during that period and was having stomach discomfort at night.

Savannah has a history of gastrointestinal issues, such as lactose intolerance and frequent constipation, which have required her to take medication. She is very aware of how she feels—"perhaps too much," her parents note—as she is constantly assessing how her stomach feels. In the middle of the fifth grade, Savannah had a 24-hour stomach virus that caused her to have gastrointestinal problems which took three months to recover from. She vomited three times over a few hours on day one of the virus. Within the first week following the virus, she was hesitant to eat. For several weeks after that, her hesitance increased.

Shortly after the vomiting episode, her parents noticed that Savannah had stopped eating and drinking regularly. She was so afraid of vomiting that she stopped eating breakfast "so I won't have an upset stomach and throw up at school." It wasn't long before Savannah stopped eating lunch as well. She was also fearful that her parents wouldn't be there to help her if she did get sick, saying, "What if throw up? How will you help me? What if I can't get a hold of you?" Already very thin, Savannah was losing weight from not eating. She began to become scared and angry before school and soon refused to go. She was clearly in distress and went from saying things like, "Why me?" to being angry, critical, negative, and depressed. At one point, Savannah stated that she'd rather be dead than have to vomit ever again.

What Neighborhood Is Savannah In?

What is going on for Savannah? Just as we did for Patrick, let's use some simple questions and answers to try to figure out how to help her. Again, this will help you decide the best way to set up a plan for your child.

> Q: What are Savannah's primary symptoms and behaviors?
> A: Fear of getting sick and vomiting, hyper-awareness of body, emotional outbursts, reduced eating, school refusal

> Q: What are some primary stressors?
> A: GI/stomach issues, vomiting

> Q: What possible anxiety neighborhoods is she in?
> A: Worry, specific phobia (fear of vomiting)

> Q: What strategies can be used to help her?
> A: Teach her about the fight or flight response; help her learn about the Worry Monster and what he is telling her; challenge and change her thinking; practice eating

Helping Savannah Fight the Worry Monster

As with Patrick, Savannah and her parents needed to use several strategies to help her fight her Worry Monster. As you can guess, Savannah first had to understand how the Worry Monster was responsible for how she was feeling. She learned about the amygdala, the role of adrenaline and how it made her body feel, the fight or flight response, and how she needed to use her thinking brain to overpower her emotional brain.

Savannah's parents were very involved in helping her "out-think" the Worry Monster. After learning about how the Worry Monster operates, as well as already knowing about the fight or flight response, they continually talked to Savannah about how the Worry Monster was making her body feel. They became quite skilled at talking to their daughter about what the Worry Monster was doing to her. Through this kind of questioning, it became apparent that the Worry Monster was telling Savannah two very simple but scary things.

Identifying Savannah's Worrisome Thinking

Dan: "What is the Worry Monster telling you when you feel scared?"

Savannah: "That it might happen again. If I eat, I will throw up again."

Being bright and perceptive, Savannah easily took to the idea of being smarter than the Worry Monster, and she liked the idea that the Worry Monster was "dumb." She practiced changing her worrisome thoughts and also talking back to the Worry Monster.

Challenging and Changing Savannah's Thinking

Dan: "What can you say to the Worry Monster when he tells you those lies?"

Savannah: "Just because my stomach feels uncomfortable, that doesn't mean I will vomit. The Worry Monster is just a bully who is trying to trick me. So what if I throw up?"

Through our conversations, Savannah also learned that all of the Worry Monster's thinking was based in the future and that if she focused on the present, the here and now, she always felt fine. Savannah immediately achieved several victories against the Worry Monster. She still had her fear of vomiting, but she started eating regularly again. And as she continued to work her plan, her fear of vomiting faded. She became less emotional, and happiness returned to her life.

However, as we saw with Patrick, the Worry Monster can be persistent and can come back for a visit now and then to see if his strategies still work. Sometimes this happens when there is a life stressor like a transition to a new school. Other times it occurs as a result of pre-adolescence or adolescence, when hormones are surging and brain chemistry is changing. And other times it happens when people forget about the Worry Monster and stop doing the things that made him go away in the first place, like realize his words are lies! About six months after we began working to fight the Worry Monster, he came back to Savannah with a vengeance, giving her one panic attack and then another. He had found his way back in.

He once again started to bully Savannah and got her to think: "My stomach feels weird. I might throw up. Remember how bad it was last time?"

The Worry Monster made Savannah so scared that she was afraid to go to school. He convinced her that she would vomit at school, that she wouldn't be able to handle it, and that her parents wouldn't be there to help her. Savannah stopped eating again, and there were daily meltdowns about going to school, with Savannah often refusing to go. It was clear that the Worry Monster had a tight grip on this young girl, and she needed her team to help her.

We developed a plan in which Savannah's teacher and principal were informed about the Worry Monster and how he was telling Savannah that she might vomit, thereby keeping her from going to school. Her principal became Savannah's "go to" person when the Worry Monster was making her scared, and her teacher understood that there might be times when Savannah needed to leave the classroom to talk to the principal without having to answer a lot of questions about it. And her parents needed to fight the Worry Monster for Savannah by insisting that she go to school, even when she didn't feel she could. This was no small feat and took a *ton* of courage from Savannah's parents. Parents often have to make their kids do things while their child is crying, begging, and pleading for them not to do this to them. It can be extremely painful to watch your child suffer and feel that you are contributing to the pain. It is important to remember, however, and to tell your child that you are doing your job to help her conquer the Worry Monster and not let him run her life. That is what Savannah's parents had to do, and it was very hard.

Reinforcing the Battle Plan

What follows is the plan that everyone agreed to. Savannah wanted this plan to work, but she was still scared, and the Worry Monster wouldn't stop putting doubts in her head.

- ✔ Go to school at all costs!

- ✔ Enlist school personnel—have a "go to" person—to support her at school.

- ✔ Carry a cell phone for calling her parents if she does get sick.

- ✔ Challenge the Worry Monster's thinking ("So what?").

- ✔ Remember that eating is healthy and that vomiting helps us survive (it gets rid of the bad stuff).

- ✔ Focus on the present—everything is fine right now!

- ✔ Read to distract herself.

Savannah and her parents needed to dig deep, and with tremendous courage, Savannah returned to school. She used her cell phone to text and call her parents from the principal's office when she was scared. At first, she would miss entire classes. But it wasn't long before she only needed to stay in the office for about 15 minutes before returning to her classroom. Savannah mounted victory after victory against the Worry Monster, eventually not needing to go to the principal's office or to call her parents at all.

Over time, Savannah reported only vaguely thinking about vomiting, but even when she did, it didn't scare her anymore. She still knows that the Worry Monster is always lurking and may not be far away—may even try to come back for a visit. However, she also knows how he messes with her and that it is very important that she not let him convince her that she can't or shouldn't go to school. In addition, Savannah knows that she has a plan and a strong team to support her.

Drew

Now I want to tell you about Drew, who is 12 and in seventh grade. Drew's story shows how elaborate and detailed an understanding a child can have regarding the monsters, how they work, and how they can be outsmarted.

Drew is a bright, kind, and conscientious person. He is a strong student and excels in all of the sports he plays. However, his parents reported that he didn't step on lines or touch corners. They also noticed that he tapped door jambs and opened and closed books repetitively. Despite having an A+ in six out of his seven classes, he worried about his school performance and felt that he needed to get the "perfect" grade. He found his advanced math class easy but said that English and history were more challenging for him because there is "no certainty" in those subjects.

Drew sometimes had different numbers in his head that represented certain things to him—for example, 3 was for sports over the weekend, and 5 was the smart number. Drew (encouraged by the OCD Monster) created a system of rules for using the numbers, and he believed that he needed to follow those rules to think "correctly." As an example, he believed that he needed to think about the number 5 when he was opening and closing his backpack. He also felt that he needed to erase a word he was writing if he wasn't thinking correctly as he wrote it or else he feared that he would turn into a bad kid, like others in his class who were poor students and got in trouble.

As you probably have guessed by now, I talked with Drew about the fight or flight response and how our scary or anxious thoughts activate our survival response. I then told him about the Worry Monster and the OCD Monster and how both of those monsters seemed to be ganging up on him to make him worry and do things he didn't want to do. Drew immediately took to this language, saying, "It's a pretty tricky monster." He said that the OCD Monster first came to him when he was in sixth-grade math, when he "needed something to do to reassure myself."

Identifying Drew's Worrisome Thinking

Dan: "What does the Worry Monster tell you?"

Drew: "If I get a lower grade, it might lead to more lower grades. My teacher will look down on my abilities. Other people won't think I'm as smart as they thought at first. I may never be able to get an A+ again."

Changing Drew's Thinking

Dan: "How can you change your thinking? What can you tell the Worry and OCD Monsters so they don't trick you?"

Drew came up with the following new thoughts to counter the Worry Monster: "Not getting an A on an assignment will affect my grade but not my future test scores. My teacher may wonder what happened, but it really doesn't matter to her. Other people aren't going to think any different of me for it. But I most likely will do well anyway because I know how to study."

Setting Up a Behavior Plan

I taught Drew about response inhibition and the importance of not doing what the OCD Monster told him to do. He decided that he would start by resisting erasing words when he was writing and also not doing things the number of times the OCD Monster told him to. It was important for me to give Drew permission to select only one or two things to work on since he was a high achiever and put a lot of pressure on himself to excel.

Drew was able to earn some initial victories over the monsters. He reported that he was able to resist erasing words, that he stopped repeatedly opening and closing books, and that he resisted having to touch things a certain number times. In fact, Drew started getting irritated at the monsters for making him do things he didn't want to do and for making him use so much mental energy. He added some new challenging thinking:

- ✔ "Why would I want to do that?"
- ✔ "I'm not going to worry about that!"

As we continued to talk about the Worry and OCD Monsters, Drew started to gain an understanding of how they work together to mess with him. One day we discovered that there was actually a third monster, the Perfectionism Monster, that often joined in as well. Drew explained to me about how these three monsters worked in tandem against him.

Drew: *The OCD Monster and the Perfectionism Monster team up. The OCD Monster is the muscle, and the Perfectionist Monster is the brains. He comes up with the ideas about being perfect, and the OCD Monster puts them to use.*

Dan: *Where does the Worry Monster come in?*

Drew: *The Worry Monster starts everything off because if you don't worry, you can't be a perfectionist. They all target your weaknesses. I thought it was weird why I did all this stuff, but now I know why.*

Dan: *How do you think you can outsmart them?*

Drew: *I know the three different monsters, and I have to separate them. If you keep the three of them apart, even though they are naturally bonded, you can fight them separately. The OCD Monster is going to make me erase words. The Perfectionist Monster wants me to stay the same person and tells me that if I don't do what the OCD Monster says, I'm not going to be who I am. The Worry Monster is going to tell me to hurry up and not erase so I won't run out of time. He makes it seem like he is my friend when he is actually a double agent, since he tries to force me to do it but makes me think he is on my side.*

Dan: *You really have these guys figured out. I'll bet you know what you need to say to them to take away their power.*

Drew: *Yes! For the OCD Monster, I can say, "This is outrageous! You can't make me do that!" To the Perfectionist Monster, I can say, "No matter what, I am going to be who I am." Finally, to the Worry Monster, I can say, "We both know you're not trying to help me!"*

Drew's Toolbox

Drew felt that he needed an arsenal of statements to say to the monsters, as well as strategies to fight them. We came up with the following:

- ✔ "Bring it on!"
- ✔ "So what?"
- ✔ Push the thought away and ignore it.
- ✔ Do the opposite of what the monster says.
- ✔ Remember that I have stood up against them before.

Drew's parents were also taught about the monsters and how they attack their son, but Drew really wanted to be independent in his battles, only asking for his parents' help when he needed it. They respected his need for independence and offered their support. They worked on being patient with him when he engaged in his rituals or was unable to transition to the next task and appeared tense. They learned to ask, "Is a monster visiting?" as a way to help him become aware that he could use one of his strategies to fight a particular behavior. Over time, Drew's parents noticed him becoming more relaxed for longer periods of time, as well as taking

schoolwork breaks and watching TV with his family, something he was previously not able to do. Drew continues to impress me with his advanced comprehension of the monsters and his courageous stand against them.

Chapter Summary

Patrick and Savannah were able to fight the Worry Monster because they were empowered with information about how their brain and body work. They were told about the Worry Monster and what he did to make them feel scared and awful. They were able to identify what the Worry Monster told them to make them feel that way and also how they could think new thoughts to change the way they felt, as well as to make the Worry Monster less powerful. They learned strategies for dealing with the worry and fear and developed a set of "tools" they could rely on when the monster came to visit. They also learned that they were not alone in their struggle but that they had a team to fight and ultimately tame the monster.

Drew benefited from learning similar information about his brain and body and the role of his thoughts in making him feel tense and worried. He used his advanced thinking abilities to take his understanding of the monsters to a new level.

Each set of parents played a key role in their child's plan. They learned the language about the monsters and talked to their child about them. They asked questions to help their child find creative ways to outsmart the monsters' thinking. They supported their child in taking steps and practicing behaviors to weaken the monsters and to help their child gain victories over them. By understanding the way the monsters worked, the parents were empowered to help their child make positive changes. In the case of Drew's parents, they respected his adolescent desire to be independent and allowed him the space to fight the monsters on his own, supporting him when he asked for help. Finally, knowing how to keep some tools in the toolbox to use when the monsters showed up helped these parents gain confidence in helping their children. You will be able to help your child with these tools as well.

Things to Remember

- ✔ Patrick, Savannah, and Drew learned how their Worry, OCD, and Perfectionism Monsters worked and then took steps to fight them.

- ✔ They became aware of what the monsters told them and learned to challenge and replace their thoughts with different thoughts.

- ✔ They engaged in behaviors that made them stronger and made the monsters weaker.

- ✔ They developed a plan and had a toolbox of strategies to use against the monsters.

- ✔ They gained confidence as they mounted their victories.

- ✔ Parental support was key in helping them work their plan.

Things to Do

- ✔ Get ready to make a plan to fight your child's Worry Monster!

CHAPTER 10

Making a Plan to Tame the Worry Monster

When you change the way you look at things, the things you look at change.

~ Wayne Dyer

It is now time to make your battle plan and turn your worrier into a warrior. The Worry Monster must be stopped, banished, or at least tamed! Your job is to help your child understand how the Worry Monster works and let him know that you are going to do this with him because it takes a whole team to fight that big bully. As you now know, when the Worry Monster succeeds in having your child avoid the feared thing, it only reinforces the fear and makes it stronger. Therefore, our goal is to face the Worry Monster, conquer him, and render him powerless. You are going to do this by helping your child learn about how his great big thinking brain (frontal cortex) can override his smaller, emotional brain (amygdala). You are going to teach your child about the simple thinking techniques of identifying and changing his thinking, as well as engaging in practice sessions to slowly overcome his fears. You are also going to help him develop a toolbox of strategies that he can use at any time.

Making and Working the Plan

I have broken everything that we have discussed in this book so far into nine simple steps. You may want to go through each step, or you may find that after doing the first few steps, you can skip a few to focus on the ones that are most relevant for your child. That is fine! Don't let the Worry Monster tell you that you are doing it wrong. By now, you know the key elements of fighting the Worry Monster: teach your child about the brain, the body, and the Worry Monster, and then develop thinking and behavior strategies to outsmart him.

Your plan can be creative and integrative with the steps that follow. The strategies listed in the previous chapters are meant to be a "menu" of choices. You do not need to use all of them. Try the ones that you think will work, and if they don't work, try others. The most important thing is to make the monster go away! Remember, your child will likely need you to remind her of the strategies at every step—breathe, focus on the present, use positive self-talk, change her thinking—until she says, "I know, I know already!" If you hear this or a similar phrase, you are doing your job well.

Step 1: Teach Your Child about the Brain

As I explained in earlier chapters, you are going to teach your child about the following important facts:

- ✔ How "fight or flight" and the survival response works

- ✔ What the amygdala is and how it runs our personal in-body security system that is designed to keep us alive

- ✔ What adrenaline is and how it is sent through our body to make us run fast and fight hard

- ✔ Why our body feels the way it does when we are nervous, worried, or scared

- ✔ That our thoughts are responsible for triggering our amygdala and sending adrenaline through our body

- ✔ That if we change our thinking, our feelings will change, too

✔ That if we practice something we are afraid of over and over, we won't be afraid of it anymore

Step 2: Identify Body Feelings

This is the first step in helping your child become aware of where he feels anxiety in his body (e.g., head, chest, stomach, throat) and how this is his indicator that the Worry Monster is paying a call and picking on him. Helpful questions include:

✔ Where do you feel it in your body?

✔ What happens when you feel nervous or scared?

✔ What are your warning signs?

✔ How do you know when you are scared or worried?

If your child is unable to answer these questions when he is not worried or scared, ask him again when he *is* experiencing the worry or fear. This tends to be more effective when the worry or fear is at a low level or just starting rather than when he is very scared or worried. You may also point out to your child that when he is nervous, you notice certain things about his behavior. This can help him increase his sense of awareness.

Step 3: Externalize the Problem

This is the point at which you are going to introduce your child to the Worry Monster (if you haven't already). Here are the key points to discuss:

✔ The Worry Monster is a bully who is responsible for making you (and all of us) think worrisome and scary thoughts.

✔ The Worry Monster's job is to keep you from enjoying life. He gets joy from picking on children (and adults) and making them worried and scared.

✔ The Worry Monster is both dumb and smart. He is dumb because he uses the same strategy over and over. He tells people that bad things are going to happen even though he can't really make them happen. (He lies about this all the time.) He is smart because he hides and uses the same strategies over and over, and most people don't realize he's there. (He is very sneaky and can creep up on us.)

✔ Show your child the picture of the Worry Monster. Let her see how silly and pathetic he looks. Laugh at him together.

✔ Talk with your child about the scene in *The Wizard of Oz* in which the true nature of the Wizard is revealed, and discuss how the characters became strong and fearless when they realized that the Wizard was not powerful and was just tricking them—just like the Worry Monster does.

✔ You and your child are now going to work together as a team to drive the Worry Monster out of your child's life. The more you and your child talk about the Worry Monster and team up against him, the sooner he will go away.

Step 4: Make a Worry List

Making a worry list is more fun than one would think, especially if you do it as a family.[37] But whether this becomes a family activity or something your child does with just you, the goal is for you and your child to make an exhaustive list of *everything* he worries about. It is basically a brainstorming session. Remind your child that the Worry Monster doesn't like us to talk about him or how he works, so the more you put on the list, the better.

Once you have made the list of worries, ask your child to apply a scare rating to each one to rate how it makes him feel using the following scale:

✔ *1-3 Mild Discomfort*: Uncomfortable and apprehensive
✔ *4-7 Moderate Discomfort*: Scared and anxious
✔ *8-10 Severe Discomfort*: Very scared and anxious (panic)

Teach your child about how his rating will tell him which things are scariest and which are the least scary. Once you have done this, put the worries and fears in order starting with the most powerful (severe) at the top and going down to the least powerful (mild). You have just created your priority list of which worries and fears to tackle first. (Start with the easy ones to build your child's confidence.)

Step 5: Make a Success Ladder

Making a success ladder is optional at this point. You can either use the ranked worry list that you made, or you can choose a behavior from the worry list and make a success ladder out of it by breaking it down into baby steps, with the ultimate fear or goal at the top of the ladder and the least scary behavior at the bottom.

You will need to decide whether your child is able to start with a single fear like riding an escalator or whether the task needs to be broken into parts so that she can gain confidence by systematically becoming used to each baby step along the way to conquering her fear.

Step 6: Identify Worrisome and Fearful Thinking

For this step, you again must talk to your child about how the Worry Monster tells him (and all of us) things that make us worry and scared. I know this sounds repetitive, but it is important to keep talking about this over and over (like practice) until your child is comfortable with and accepting of this way of thinking about his worries and fears.

Take out the worry list, and tell your child that you and he are going to start making the Worry Monster weak by uncovering the monster's strategies and tactics. You are going to expose his secrets by writing down what he tells your child to make him worried and scared. Read each worry, and ask your child what the Worry Monster tells him about each one. Again, make as exhaustive a list as possible. For example:

Worries	What the Worry Monster Tells Me
Being left alone	I might get left at school. Something bad might happen to my mom.
Sleeping alone	Someone might break into our house. I might have a nightmare.
Taking tests	What if I forget everything? What if I fail?

Step 7: Change and Modify Thinking

Now that you and your child have a list of worries that includes the things the Worry Monster says, it is time to teach your child about how the Worry Monster makes her think in specific ways that make her worried and scared. This is when you can start to teach your child about the different types of thinking errors discussed in Chapter 5. Of course, you can skip this part with younger children or any child not ready or willing to do this activity. It is important to gauge your child's interest.

Take the top one to three worries or fears that your child is willing to work on. Remember, you can use incentives if you need to. Go back to the list where you wrote what the Worry Monster tells you, and next to those thoughts, write down new thoughts that are healthier and more realistic. Your list might look like this:

Old Thought (What the Worry Monster Tells Me)	New Thought
I might get left at school.	I have never been left before.
Something bad might happen to my mom.	My mom is strong and can take care of herself.
Someone might break into our house.	We always lock our doors and windows.
I might have a nightmare.	Nightmares are scary, but I am always okay when they are over.
What if I forget everything?	I never forget everything.
What if I fail?	I studied for the test. So what if I fail?

Here are some useful questions to ask your child, both while you are helping to change her thoughts during this exercise and in real time when the Worry Monster is visiting:

✔ What are you thinking?

✔ What is the thinking error involved?

✔ Is the thought realistic? Is it true? Can you state evidence to prove that it's true or not true?

✔ How can you think about this topic differently?

✔ What can you think instead that is more true and realistic?

Particularly at first, you will need to help your child come up with contradictory evidence to her fears and alternative ways to think. Over time, your child will be able to do this, first on her own with your prompting, and eventually without needing you to prompt her at all.

Step 8: Practice, Practice, Practice!

This is where the real work comes in. You, with the help of your child (depending on age, interest, and motivation), are going to create behavioral practice activities designed to tackle the Worry Monster head on. Remember, your child can either work on a fear in its entirety, like walking into school on his own, or accomplish it in steps as part of a success ladder, in which he starts by walking part of the way to the school by himself.

They key principle here is to start with something that your child can handle with very little fear, such as waving to a neighbor while driving in the car. Your child needs an early victory to gain confidence in his ability to fight the Worry Monster. Once your child has had some success, do the same victorious behavior a few more times until it becomes boring and unnecessary. The goal is to have zero feelings of anxiety when engaging in each behavioral step forward. Zero anxiety is a crystal clear way to gauge when your child is ready for the next step in his success ladder and/or is ready to tackle his next scare step.

As I said earlier, reinforcement and rewards are sometimes needed to help your child take the steps necessary to slowly defeat the Worry Monster and mount victories against him. Include your child in the reward program, since you are going to need rewards that are motivating to him. Remember, the reward needs to be strong enough to help your child take a courageous step against the Worry Monster.

One family I know created a "Victory Chart." The chart serves two purposes for them: first, it's where they list their goals, and second, it's also where they record the fears or worries that they have conquered, and it reminds them of all of the negative things they have overcome. The chart hangs below a picture that shows how the amygdala makes us worry. Both the picture and the Victory Chart are posted on the back of their son's bedroom door, and he refers to it often. Other families take a picture of the Worry Monster and put stickers, stars, or pushpins over him every time there is a victory until the Worry Monster is covered and disappears. If you want to do this, you can find a full-color version of Worry Monster at http://bit.ly/ParentWarrior or http://bit.ly/TheWorryMonster. The image is available as a pdf file that you can print out and use with your child.

Step 9: Develop a Coping Toolbox

Regardless of whether your child conquers the Worry Monster quickly or takes baby steps to defeat him, she will benefit from having a personalized toolbox to help her take on the Worry Monster when he shows up. This toolbox usually consists of strategies like deep breathing, understanding where she feels the worry (i.e., her body indicators), knowing her triggers (i.e., new situations), common phrases to challenge her thinking, and activities that distract and relax her.

You can help your child design her toolbox by asking her:

✔ How do you know when the Worry Monster is visiting?
✔ What can you do to combat him?
✔ What thinking strategies should you use?
✔ What distracts you from worry and fear?
✔ What helps you feel more confident and relaxed?

Here is a list of some tools that you and your child can choose from. Feel free to add to this list:

✔ Take deep breaths.
✔ Focus on the present moment.
✔ Use positive self-talk ("I can do this!").

✔ Ask yourself what you are thinking.

✔ Change your thinking.

✔ Talk back to the Worry Monster ("Take a hike, you cowardly bully!").

✔ Ignore the Worry Monster ("So what?").

✔ Distract yourself with another activity.

✔ Exercise.

✔ Seek support from a friend, parent, or teacher.

✔ Use your worry box.

✔ Reserve your worries for worry time later.

Your child will learn that she can bring her toolbox with her everywhere. Nobody will see it, especially the Worry Monster. Knowing that she always has these tools available will help her feel more confident and ready for the Worry Monster anytime and anywhere.

Working with Your Child's Teacher and School

As you saw in Savannah's case in the previous chapter, her teacher, principal, and other school staff played a key role in helping her tame her Worry Monster and get back to school. Some of your child's worries and fears may be independent of school, yet others might be directly connected to it, such as a fear of being away from parents, test performance, speaking or reading in front of the class, or changing clothes and participating in PE. Remember that our children's survival response often looks more like a behavior problem—defiance, refusal, emotional meltdowns—which masks the actual reason for the response: fear.

Time and time again, I have seen school staff go from frustration to compassion when they are told about a child's worry, anxiety, and fear. With compassion comes a desire to help a child tame his Worry Monster. That's why it is critical to involve your child's teacher and other school personnel when necessary. Worry and fear is nothing to be ashamed of, and modeling this attitude for your child by talking to his teacher about it shows that you are not ashamed of it either (although most children don't want anyone to know about it).

Here is a short list of topics you can discuss with your child's teacher:

- ✔ Explain the nature of your child's worry or fear (i.e., speaking in front of the class).

- ✔ Explain your plan for how you are working on the fear at home, including describing who the Worry (Perfectionist/OCD) Monster is. You can discuss baby steps, practice, etc.

- ✔ Explain how the monster affects your child and what the teacher is likely to see in the classroom.

- ✔ Ask what ideas the teacher has to support your child in managing his anxiety and taking steps to tame his monster.

- ✔ Create a joint reward system to motivate your child to take steps against his monster and mount victories.

- ✔ Determine a communication method to exchange information about significant events (positive and negative) at home and school.

As you have learned by now, it takes a team to drive away the Worry Monster (and his friends). Often, your child's teacher and other school personnel are a necessary and helpful part of that team.

And Poof, He's Gone!

There you have it. You have just learned the secret to fighting and taming the Worry Monster. He is no longer a mystery. He is no longer a threat. He is no longer lurking in the shadows. Well, he's still lurking, but no longer in the shadows. You and your child have exposed him. You know all, or at least most, of his tricks and have several strategies to systematically conquer him and render him powerless. Look at him; he's getting so small and puny! Poor Worry Monster. He needs to go away and find someone else to pick on.

Poof!

Things to Remember

- ✔ You don't need to do every step of the plan. Make a plan that you think will work so that your child can have a victory.

- ✔ Observe what parts of the plan your child identifies with (body feelings, changing thinking, practicing behaviors), and emphasize those steps.

- ✔ Remember to focus on small, incremental steps and victories.

- ✔ Use Worry Monster language when talking about worries and fears.

- ✔ Continually highlight the victories and positive steps your child is taking against the Worry Monster.

Things to Do

- ✔ Make a plan with your child.

- ✔ Work the plan.

- ✔ Make your worrier a warrior.

- ✔ Banish the Worry Monster!

CHAPTER 11

Fine Tuning and Healthy Habits

The trick is to enjoy life. Don't wish away your days waiting for better ones ahead.

~ Marjorie Hinckley

Of course you hope that you will see some immediate positive results from your battle plan, and to some degree, that is realistic. Your child should be able to at least try, with the help of incentives, the behaviors at the bottom of her worry list or success ladder—the ones that are least scary. From my experience, I can say that some children make surprisingly fast progress, but other children may be either too scared and/or not willing to take any chances to chase the Worry Monster away.

It may be helpful to think about Dr. Liebgold's metaphor of climbing a mountain to visualize the quest and the challenge of fighting worry and fear:[38]

✔ Initially, it looks attainable.

✔ It requires specific training.

✔ It must be done one step at a time.

✔ Each step, no matter how small, brings you closer to the top.

✔ Sometimes you slide back and have to re-climb the same area.

✔ Sometimes you go fast, and sometimes you go slow, depending on the difficulty of the terrain.

✔ Sometimes you fail and have to choose an alternate path.

✔ It is hard to do and may take a long time.

✔ It takes practice, perseverance, and determination.

Ideas for Fine Tuning the Plan

Sometimes you and your child need to adjust or fine-tune your plan. Here is a list of ideas and strategies to consider if your child is having trouble working the plan and taking on the Worry Monster.

Start with a Victory

Make sure you are starting small enough on the success ladder. Sometimes we get excited about helping our children conquer their fears, and we go too fast for them. Stay with the small behaviors, and do them over and over until your child is ready for another one. You will know when he's ready because the behavior practice will become "easy" and "boring." Once he's using words like that, you can ask him if he is ready for the next step on the ladder. At that point, he mostly likely will be.

Look at Your Reinforcement Plan

Remember that your child wants to avoid doing the things she fears because facing fears is scary. This means that the external reinforcement you offer needs to be powerful and enticing enough to help your child take a step toward facing her fears. It may be that the reinforcement is not powerful enough or that your child's fear is too strong. If the problem is the former, try to find an item or an event that truly motivates your child and that you are comfortable giving. If your child is too fearful to take a step, it means that you need to scale back what you are asking her to do so she can win a victory. Remember, baby steps.

My son had the same childhood fear I had of bowel movements. Thus, I knew not to make the same mistakes my parents did with me that made it a big deal that affected me for years. So first we gave him mineral oil regularly with no instructions to try to practice sitting on the toilet. There was no point in making a constipated five-year-old hate and fear the potty more. When his stools were soft again, I told him, "I know you can poop in the potty when you are ready, and one day you will be ready. No problem. So for your first three poops on the potty, we will run right out to the toy store, and you can spend $20 on whatever you want." One day he was sufficiently motivated not to ask for a diaper to poop in. He pooped in the potty, and we went and got his toy. After that he did the next two poops easily—and got his toys after each one. By the third victory, he didn't need reinforcement. He entered kindergarten the following fall without any more toilet issues and lived happily ever after—in this regard, that is.

~ mother of a warrior

Try Working on a Different Worry or Fear

Sometimes a child just has trouble facing a particular fear and will have more success tackling another one. If that's the case, go back to your child's worry list, and choose another fear to work on. Again, start with an easy first step so your child can win a victory.

Try a Different Thinking Strategy

Sometimes the thinking strategies you come up with don't resonate with your child, or they simply don't work. Look at the ones you have created (i.e., "I don't need to worry about my mom not coming to pick me up because my mom *always* comes to get me") and try a new one (i.e., "My mom will be here soon"). Sometimes just a slight rewording can be helpful.

Distraction

Occasionally you just need to come up with a way for your child to be distracted from her fear. This can be reading, limited screen time, riding a bike, or whatever takes her mind off of the worry and fear. While this strategy doesn't directly face the fear, it does help the child *live* and *do* instead of sit around and worry.

Add More Tools

If your child is having trouble taking steps and engaging in practice sessions, he may need more tools in his toolbox. Be creative, as virtually anything that helps your child battle the Worry Monster can go in the toolbox. Your child may need to practice some deep breathing, carry a picture he drew of himself destroying the Worry Monster in his pocket, or text you every time the Worry Monster is visiting.

The Worry Monster does not like to be defeated, so he hangs on for as long as he can. The additional strategies in this chapter should help you and your child gain some traction against him and progressively get results.

Diet and Exercise

Diet and exercise continue to prove to be important aspects of our mental and physical health. When we do not take care of these health essentials, it opens the door for the Worry Monster to walk in. The acronym HALT—Hungry, Angry, Lonely, Tired—is useful for thinking of the underlying reasons your child might get visited by the Worry Monster and/or have negative emotions and behaviors.[39] Most parents know how ineffective it is to try to reason with a child who is hungry or angry or lonely or tired. You have to take care of those situations first.

With regard to diet, it is important that your child eat a steady dose of protein throughout the day. Many kids, particularly intense and worried ones, experience temporary low blood sugar, and during that time they have difficulty concentrating and are likely to feel anxious. This condition typically occurs a few hours after a meal or early in the morning when glucose levels are at their lowest, and it resembles the symptoms of anxiety, which include feeling light-headed, weak, and irritable, as well as sweating and having a racing heart.[40] It is not uncommon for some children to experience low glucose levels several times throughout the day and incorrectly attribute their symptoms to anxiety.

If you think your child shows signs of hypoglycemia, you can create a simple test to find out. Make sure your child has protein for breakfast (i.e., cereal with milk, an egg, a peanut butter sandwich, some cheese). Then have your child take a protein snack mid-morning (cheese stick, peanut butter crackers, yogurt), protein again for lunch, a mid-afternoon protein snack, and protein again at dinner. If your child's mood swings disappear with this protein regimen, you can be pretty confident that he experiences temporary hypoglycemia and needs the mid-day protein boost. However, it is not uncommon these days for children to have food allergies that require specialized diets. If your child has particular food allergies, you may need to give him alternatives like soy butter instead of peanut butter, organic beef jerky, or organic goat cheese.

The following substances are ones that your child (and you) should try to stay away from because the effects of ingesting them actually mimic the effects of adrenaline and can make people feel anxious: caffeine, energy drinks, nicotine, and alcohol.[41] In addition to avoiding those, regular exercise will help in fighting the Worry Monster and keeping him at bay. Exercise burns adrenaline and makes the heart less sensitive to it.[42] If it's not already a part of your child's daily routine, add daily exercise to your child's plan, and let him know that not only is it good for his body, but it will help render the Worry Monster powerless. Exercise can include any number of activities that your child may enjoy: swimming, shooting baskets, hiking, soccer, dodgeball, tennis, martial arts, jump roping, rock climbing, bicycling, dancing, gymnastics, yoga, and more.

> *After I swim or play tennis, I feel calm. I am a lot happier after I exercise.*
>
> ~ nine-year-old warrior

Sleep

How much quality sleep do children and adolescents need? The National Sleep Foundation recommends that three- to five-year-olds get 11-13 hours a night, five- to 12-year-olds get 10-11 hours per night, and teens get 9.25 hours per night (although some do fine with 8.5 hours).[43] We need sleep to think clearly, to learn, and to effectively manage our emotions and behaviors. As the philosopher Friedrich Nietzsche said, "When we are tired, we are attacked by ideas we conquered long ago," and the Worry Monster certainly will try to take advantage of us when we are hungry, angry, lonely, or tired.

> *When I am learning something new, I am afraid I will never get it. I get emotional. I hit myself. I say I am a disappointment. Sometimes I say I hate myself and I want to die. Usually I am tired, and once I rest, I am better the next day.*
>
> ~ eight-year-old warrior

For a better sleep experience, these tactics help:[44]

- ✔ Plan a consistent time for going to sleep, seven days a week.

- ✔ Reduce light exposure in the hour before sleep, especially TV/cell phone/computer screens.

- ✔ Remove all sources of light from the bedroom (unless a soft light is needed to keep the Worry Monster away).

- ✔ Cool down. Body temperature drops to fall asleep (a warm bath or shower actually facilitates this by moving blood circulation closer to skin and away from the body's organs).

- ✔ Eliminate exposure to noise or distractions that could cause waking.

- ✔ If you wake during the night, avoid turning on lights.

- ✔ Practice a ritual for preparing to sleep (for example, read a book, take a hot bath or shower).

What If the Worry Monster Still Won't Go Away?

If you have tried the strategies presented in this book and your child's Worry Monster is still having a significant impact on her ability to function and enjoy life, it is time to seek professional help. Also, if the strategies in this book aren't effective, it may mean that your child's worry and fear are too severe for her to manage her thoughts well enough to engage in a plan, and/or there is more to your child's story, like possibly a learning, developmental, or emotional issue or other environmental stressor involved. Sometimes, too, children just need to hear about what they need to do from an expert who is not their parent, even though that person may prescribe the same things you already have tried.

I recommend finding a mental health professional with experience and expertise in helping children overcome anxiety. I also recommend that you ask what approaches he or she uses. While there are several effective theoretical approaches to working with children, I advise working with a professional who uses cognitive behavioral strategies as part of his or her approach.

Some parents find themselves in the difficult situation of having to consider medication for their child because their child's worry and fear is significantly handicapping her life, and therapy or counseling doesn't seem to be working quickly enough. In that case, medication—at least for a short while, until the child can learn self-management skills—may be needed to help the child gain some relief in order to work her plan. Finding a developmental or behavioral pediatrician or a child psychiatrist who specializes in anxiety is important if you find yourself in this situation, and you will want a person who recognizes that although medication may help reduce the symptoms, cognitive and behavioral approaches will build the foundational and ongoing skills and strategies that will reduce and eliminate the anxiety. Even if you do decide to try medication, it is still important to continue counseling and working the plan that you have made with your child.

> *Our daughter was resistant to trying behavioral interventions, but she had a crisis that created a lot of anxiety for her, which soon increased into OCD and then turned into depression. I'm a mental health professional myself, but I took her to two other professionals, and they agreed that in her case, even though she was resistant, we could use behavioral tools at home. So I got creative and outsmarted her. I brought a class on the brain into her school; she and her peers loved it, and they all learned tools to use to fight their negative emotions.*
>
> *I watched my daughter closely to find out what she loved most—it was music and performing. We tried out several music programs and teachers until she found her passion. Then she had a reason to face her fears because she wanted to stop beating herself up as a musician. So she became very motivated to change her behaviors.*
>
> *We also worked where she was open to making changes. I introduced her to tea and soft music, and these became beloved self-soothing mechanisms. She gave up eating napkins and ice.*

I told her, "I'm teaching you things so you can teach your friends," and that worked. She came to realize that she had more coping skills than her friends had, which motivated her to keep learning new skills. We found ways to make the work fun. We ridiculed and raged at her anxiety, which we called "the world's worst roommate in your head; tell her to SHUT UP." I found ways to make her laugh, and our closeness grew and grew. It eventually became her habit to turn to me when she was upset.

So don't lose hope when you have a resistant child. I had a very resistant, bright, independent eight-year-old, and now I have a teen who is close to her mom and owns with pride her "toolbox." We have some tough conversations about when "it's time to add another tool," but these end well now. It's a journey, and she understands in a deep way how worth it the journey is—and it's a joy that we are on it together.

~ mother of a warrior

Things to Remember

- ✔ The Worry Monster does not want to go away and can be very stubborn and tricky.

- ✔ Small victories are a step in the right direction.

- ✔ Sometimes adding a new tool or strategy results in a victory.

- ✔ Diet, exercise, and sleep are important for keeping the Worry Monster away.

- ✔ Counseling can be very helpful when the Worry Monster won't stop bullying.

- ✔ Medication might be an option if none of the strategies in this book work for your child, but should be used in conjunction with cognitive-behavioral therapy approaches.

Things to Do

- ✔ Try a new strategy or tool to trick the Worry Monster.

- ✔ Focus on one small step in your plan.

- ✔ Change the reinforcements if current ones aren't working.

- ✔ Make sure that your child exercises daily, and be mindful of what your child is eating and drinking.

- ✔ Help your child get a good night's sleep.

- ✔ Seek professional help if the Worry Monster won't go away and your child continues to be negatively impacted.

CHAPTER 12

Special Groups:
Gifted, Twice-Exceptional (2e), ADHD, and Other Learning and Processing Challenges

Neither comprehension nor learning can take place in an atmosphere of anxiety.

~ Rose Kennedy

In my work with children and families over the years, I have found that there are groups of children who tend to be more susceptible to visits by the Worry Monster than other children. My goal in this chapter is to tell you a little about these groups and why they seem predisposed to experience worry and fear more than others. One or more of these categories may apply to your child, or perhaps none of them will. If any of them do, however, the information in this chapter will help you understand and have empathy for your child's experiences.

Gifted Children

Gifted children have advanced cognitive ability and/or talents and often show advanced development at an early age—for example, in areas such as walking, talking, reading, math, and even artistic or musical ability. Many gifted children demonstrate unusual talent or ability in just about everything they do, but some show high ability in only one area, which means that there is a broad span in the levels of their various abilities—i.e., they may excel at math but be average readers. This is called *asynchronous development*.[45] Additionally, many professionals have noticed that the brighter the child, the more likely it is that the child is unusually sensitive and intense, and also the more likely her judgment is to lag behind her intellect.

Asynchronous development, in which a child has different levels of development in different areas of functioning, can provide an easy neighborhood for the Worry Monster to move into. For example, imagine that you have an eight-year-old child who has the verbal skills of a 12-year-old, the reading abilities of a 16-year-old, the math abilities of a 10-year-old, the writing skills of a seven-year-old, and the social, emotional, and behavioral regulation abilities of a six-year-old. Do you think that this asynchrony could cause some challenges and worries?

Asynchronous development means that gifted kids can have multiple levels of development, and like most of the rest of us, they focus on their weaker areas rather than their stronger ones, discounting what comes easily to them. Because they feel their internal and external environment more intensely, they often require extra support from others to navigate their world and bring their talents to fruition.

Common Characteristics of Gifted Children

There are other traits of gifted children that can provide unlocked doors for the Worry Monster to enter through. What follows is a list of the common characteristics of gifted children. Not all gifted children will exhibit every trait on the list, but they likely will demonstrate many of them.

Most people think that brighter kids are pretty immune to worry and other troubles. However, notice the italicized characteristics; these are ones that seem to make gifted children more susceptible to the Worry Monster:[46]

✔ Rapid learners
✔ *Strong memory*
✔ Large vocabulary
✔ *Advanced comprehension of nuances*
✔ Largely self-taught
✔ *Unusual emotional depth*
✔ *Abstract/complex/logical/insightful thinking*
✔ *Idealism and sense of justice*
✔ *Intense feelings and reactions*
✔ *Highly sensitive*
✔ Long attention span and persistence
✔ *Preoccupied with own thoughts*
✔ Impatient with self and others' inabilities and slowness
✔ *Ask probing questions (able to go beyond what is taught)*
✔ Wide range of interests
✔ *Highly developed curiosity*
✔ Interest in experimenting and doing things differently
✔ *Divergent thinking (putting things together in different or unusual ways)*
✔ Keen and unusual sense of humor

As you can see, gifted kids are deep thinkers, ask probing questions, are committed to justice, and are highly emotional and sensitive. In my experience, that all leads to more questions and more feelings that inadvertently welcome the Worry Monster. But wait; there's more….

Overexcitabilities (OEs)

Kazimierz Dabrowski, a Polish psychiatrist and psychologist, studied accomplished gifted artists and performers, and he developed a theory that explains the sensitivity and intensity experienced by many gifted people. He called this tendency to be extremely sensitive and intense the *overexcitabilities* (OEs), which he described as a greater capacity to be stimulated by and respond to external and internal stimuli.[47] Dabrowski described five types of OEs. Again, notice that most of these OEs (all but perhaps psychomotor) seem to prime gifted children for more feelings of worry and anxiety.

✔ *Psychomotor*: Movement, strong drive, energy, extended bouts of activity

✔ *Intellectual*: Insatiable curiosity, thirst for knowledge, voracious appetite and capacity for intellectual effort and stimulation, intensified and accelerated mental activity

✔ *Sensual*: Heightened experiences of seeing, hearing, smelling, tasting, and touching

✔ *Imaginational*: Active imagination and fantasy life

✔ *Emotional*: Capacity for emotional depth, empathy, deeply feeling own and others' emotions

Gifted children don't necessarily have all five of the overexcitabilities, but often they have at least a few. As you can imagine, thinking deeply (about why the universe is the way it is and why there is poverty and disease), having a sensitive sensory system (for tags, textures, odors, light, and sound), having a well-developed imagination (about all of the possible things that can go wrong), and feeling your own and others' emotions deeply (including sadness and worry) can all lead to feeling nervous, uncomfortable, confused, and scared. Thus, my experience is that these overexcitabilities tend to render gifted children especially susceptible to the Worry Monster.[48]

Attentional, Learning, and Processing Disorders

Many children have challenges associated with attentional, learning, and processing disorders. These kids, in my experience, are very susceptible to the Worry Monster because of the challenges they face in the classroom and in daily life. Here is a short list of some of the more common disorders (this list is by no means exhaustive):

✔ *Attention Deficit/Hyperactivity Disorder (ADHD)*: Developmentally immature levels of inattention, hyperactivity, and impulsivity; organization and executive functioning deficits; challenges with managing emotions and behavior

✔ *Asperger's Disorder*: Challenges in engaging in a reciprocal relationship; inability or difficulty with noticing and understanding social nuances; challenges with flexible thinking; requires routine and structure with little to no surprises; challenges with managing emotions when things aren't the way they are "supposed to be"

✔ *Dyslexia*: Difficulty learning and processing written language, despite adequate intelligence, instruction, and motivation; challenges with reading, writing, and sometimes math; can include executive functioning, auditory, and rote and procedural (sequential) memory challenges

✔ *Dysgraphia*: Challenges in fine-motor functioning, which affects writing; difficulty or inability to express thoughts on paper

✔ *Sensory Integration Disorder (SID)/Sensory Processing Disorder (SPD)*: Difficulty with different sensory systems and motor systems working together (difficulty with muscle control, difficulty regulating sensory input like light or sound); sensory seeking (needs to touch and move) and/or avoiding (needs to escape and have quiet)

✔ *Central Auditory Processing Disorder (CAPD)*: Weaknesses in processing and responding to oral language; challenges in recognizing and interpreting sounds

✔ *Depression*: Chronic sad or irritable mood; hopeless about future; feels helpless in the present; irritability; apathy

✔ *Anxiety*: I think you have an idea of what this is at this point!

My experience is that depression and anxiety can either be a primary issue, or they can be a secondary issue, meaning that they are the result of other issues that are going on in a child's life. Either way, they negatively affect the child.

If you suspect that your child may be experiencing any of the challenges discussed in this chapter—or even one that isn't covered here—talk to your child's teacher, and inquire about your child's performance and behavior in the classroom. The two of you should be able to come up with a plan to help your child get over her worst fears. If time passes and things don't improve, request (in writing) that the school conduct a comprehensive assessment to determine if your child has a learning and/or processing issue. I also recommend that you seek outside consultation through a psychologist trained in identifying learning, processing, developmental, and emotional issues in children, as well as consulting with other allied professionals, such as occupational therapists for sensory processing issues.

Twice-Exceptional (2e) Children

A widespread myth about gifted individuals is that they are good at everything and have no challenges. Wrong! Gifted people can also have learning, attentional, processing, emotional, developmental, and/or physical challenges as well. Not only is this true, it is more common than most people think. Gifted children (and adults) who also have one or more learning or behavioral disorders or disabilities are commonly referred to as *twice-exceptional*, or *2e*. Their abilities are at both ends of the bell curve—they have advanced cognitive and/or academic ability on the one hand, and a challenge area, such as ADHD or anxiety, on the other.

Children and adolescents who are 2e not only have many of the gifted characteristics, they also may have difficulty with one or more of the following challenges (or reasons to worry): writing, taking tests, showing academic competence and mastery, public speaking, reading, completing schoolwork, turning in schoolwork, meeting new people, socially appropriate behavior, participating in sports, standing up for themselves, attempting new activities, tying shoes, riding a bike, driving a car, getting a job, and/or going to college.

Remember the concept of asynchronous development? If your child is 2e, that means he has super-asynchronous development—or extreme discrepancies in his abilities—and this can cause him a significant amount of worry and anxiety. Why? Bright children (and adults) tend to expect themselves to perform at their highest level for all that they do. This means that they expect their advanced development and performance to be equal across all of their abilities. However, because they are 2e or have a significant weakness, they underperform and struggle in some areas, often causing noteworthy anxiety and pain.

It is also common for bright kids to be able to compensate for their weaknesses just enough so that they perform at "grade-expected levels." Parents and teachers can miss the signs of a learning problem but also the signs of their giftedness, and these children do not receive academic support for either, both in or out of school.[49] If you are a parent of a gifted or 2e child, you will likely find it no surprise that these kids tend to be perfectionistic, with little if any tolerance for anything less than the best. This, of course, leaves a lot of room for the Worry and/or Perfectionist Monster.

Special Kids and Special Accommodations

Devon, who was diagnosed with ADHD when he was six, worries about what will happen at school. He often gets called on in class when he is not paying attention, and everyone laughs at him. He also often finds himself getting reprimanded by his teacher and not knowing what he did to get in trouble. He has developed stomachaches and anxiety because he knows something will happen that is bad, but he is not sure when it will happen or what it will be.

Letty, age five, gets nervous when she gets close to her kindergarten classroom, and she clings to her mother. She is scared of the school bell and loud noises (kids screaming) on the playground. She also hears the sounds of the overhead lights buzzing, and the noise is distracting to her. She hides in the corner when it is free time and cries. Her teachers don't know what is wrong.

Stu, age 11, refuses to write. He says it is "stupid" and a waste of time. He can talk about anything he sees or hears, but he cannot get his thoughts down on paper. When he writes, he feels "dumb" because his writing is illegible to his teacher. He dreads essays and homework and often gets oppositional and argumentative when he has an assignment.

Tish, age eight, is always nervous during reading time. She reads slowly and never has enough time to finish the assigned pages. She is always worried about getting called on to read in front of the class. She anxiously anticipates her teacher's questions and frequently asks to go the bathroom to avoid doing what she needs to do.

Oliver, age 12, gets very nervous when his teacher changes the schedule or someone doesn't follow the rules during a game. He becomes visibly upset and either lashes out or starts to yell. He doesn't understand why things need to change. When he is asked what makes him worry the most each day, he says, "Things changing."

These are just a few examples of what children with learning or processing challenges or overexcitabilities have to deal with regularly. Is it any wonder why the Worry Monster likes to bully them? He really is a relentless coward, picking on kids who already have daily challenges. You can see how having any of the challenges in our examples would make the school day (and other parts of the day) a hotbed for worry and anxiety.

Understanding whether your child is experiencing any of these challenges (including having advanced cognitive development) is vital in helping her manage her daily stress and worry. Not only will it help with understanding why she may be nervous or avoiding situations, but understanding your child's learning profile will also allow you to make accommodations in her environment that can reduce her worry. Request that your child be evaluated for an Individualized Education Program (IEP) or Section 504 Plan to receive appropriate accommodations to improve her performance and reduce her anxiety in school. Examples of accommodations that can reduce anxiety include:

- ✔ More time for tests

- ✔ Ability to take tests and work in a distraction-free environment

- ✔ Less copying and writing

- ✔ No public reading or speaking until ready to do so

- ✔ Use of a keyboard and/or voice recognition software

- ✔ Audio books

- ✔ Reduction of homework, particularly work that has been mastered

- ✔ Differentiation and acceleration in coursework for advanced areas (language arts, math, science)

When we understand why the Worry Monster picks on our kids, we can make a comprehensive plan to help them take a stand against him while giving them appropriate accommodations and support to reduce the Worry Monster's power, allowing our children greater opportunities to experience success and increased confidence.

Things to Remember

- ✔ Gifted children are sensitive and susceptible to the Worry Monster.

- ✔ Gifted kids can also have learning or processing issues that can play into their anxieties.

- ✔ All kids with learning issues, gifted or not, experience daily worries and anxiety related to their challenge area(s).

- ✔ Finding out about your child's possible learning and/or processing challenges is key to helping her not only fight the Worry Monster, but experience success and confidence in school.

✔ Understanding your child's learning and processing challenges is essential for designing an intervention and accommodation plan.

Things to Do

✔ If you are concerned about your child's learning and/or behavior, talk to her teacher.

✔ If you continue to be concerned and don't see improvement, request (in writing) that your child receive a comprehensive assessment of her learning in order to qualify for an IEP or Section 504 Plan.

✔ Seek outside consultation and evaluation from a psychologist or learning specialist who is experienced with children and adolescents.

CHAPTER 13

Do the Same Strategies Work for Adults?

Most things I worry about never happen anyway.

~ Tom Petty

Yep, this stuff works for adults, too.

I had planned to write this book for a long time. I had so many ideas to share, and I felt that the book would come rather easily, as I would simply be writing about the work I do day in and day out, as well as speak about regularly. I finally carved out a weekend away for intensive writing and was excited as the days approached. It was the Friday before the writing weekend, and guess who came to visit?

It started fairly innocuously with a little pressure in my chest and an uneasy feeling in my stomach. I shook it off and did a pretty good job of ignoring it, and I was able to focus on my clients. I came home to pack for the weekend, and the feeling was still there—subtle, but there. The feeling grew stronger on the drive and remained steady until bedtime. "Ah ha!" said the Worry Monster as I lay in bed trying to fall asleep. "It's time to attack!" And boy did he attack.

The negative thoughts came fast. "What if you don't have anything to say? What if you don't get enough done? What if you have trouble writing what you want to say? Maybe you don't know as much as you think you do." As these thoughts were running through my mind, I became very aware of the feelings that I'd been experiencing in my chest and stomach all day.

Believe it or not, I actually smiled and thought, "How funny. The Worry Monster is coming to visit me when I am preparing to write about how to get rid of him." As you know, the Worry Monster and I are pretty well-acquainted. We're not exactly best friends, but we know each other well. I took a deep breath, and then several more, and asked myself, "What am I thinking?" It was not hard to identify my thoughts. I made a mental list and then set out to change them.

Here is what my list looked like (in my mind):

Worry Monster Thought	My New Thought
"What if you don't have anything to say?"	"I always have something to say about the Worry Monster."
"What if you don't get enough done?"	"I will take one step at a time and do as much as I can."
"What if you have trouble writing what you want to say?"	"I will focus on my ideas and experiences."
"Maybe you don't know as much as you think you do."	"I have been doing this work for a long time and know enough to share my experiences with others."

As I was systematically changing my thinking, the pressure in my chest started to go away, as well as the uneasy feeling in my stomach. Once again, I was reminded how sneakily the Worry Monster works, and also how simple it is to make him go away.

If you are reading this book, you most likely spend a substantial amount of time supporting your child through difficult experiences, whether those experiences are in the real world, in the child's head, or both. By the time you have gotten to this chapter, you have learned how the brain and body work with regard to anxiety and our survival instinct, how the Worry Monster places thoughts in our children's heads to activate this alarm system, and several strategies for overpowering the Worry Monster by helping our children to change their thinking and engage in behaviors that weaken the Worry Monster's influence.

Guess what? You have also just learned how to fight your own Worry Monster, and your anxious child may have helped you do it! Sometimes we need something outside of us to help us make a substantial and courageous change. There is nothing more powerful than the love of a parent for a child. What's more, fighting our own monsters helps our children fight theirs. As I have already mentioned, fighting the Worry Monster takes courage and conviction. It takes a commitment to no longer live in and be ruled by fear. Yes, I know, this is easy to say and harder to do, but you're reading this book because you can see the effects that worry and fear have on your child's life. So why not make it a two-for-one? Help yourself while you help your child.

If you need a little more motivation to fight your Worry Monster, here it is: your child will be more motivated to fight his Worry Monster if he sees you fighting yours. You are your child's primary role model, and there is nothing more powerful than showing him how to successfully win at these battles. I have seen this time and time again in my office—and in my personal life. The child will intently listen to his parents talking about their worries and fears and what they want to do about them, and the child will step in and offer advice. Even better, an alliance is often forged: "*We* are going to make the Worry Monster disappear!"

All of this is to say that everything you have read about, learned, and practiced as you help your child with his Worry Monster completely and totally applies to adults as well. When you are feeling nervous, worried, anxious, or scared:

✔ Ask yourself what you are thinking.

✔ Ask yourself if it is true.

✔ Change your thinking so that it's more realistic. Change your self-talk about it.

✔ Engage in the behavior the Worry Monster is scaring you into not doing.

✔ Practice the behavior over and over until it's no big deal.

✔ Smile to yourself, and give yourself a high five or a fist bump because you have just earned another victory over the Worry Monster.

Bringing It Home

Dear Dr. Dan,

I've learned a lot about the Worry Monster with you and when he's giving me worries…. I've learned that the Worry Monster thinks of the thing that a good non-worry kid would say, and then he thinks the opposite and says that to you. So he gives you lots of worries. So if you just overpower him by talking about him and doing lots and lots of practice about him, you will [conquer] your Worry Monster [and have] no worries. Then when you have no worries, you can help your friends not worry…. So I think that the Worry Monster is really bad. So if you ever get the Worry Monster, you should punch him out!

~ eight-year-old warrior

You now know how the Worry Monster works. You know how he triggers the fight or flight response in your child's brain and body and how he tells your child things to make her worried and scared. However, you also know that when your child slightly alters the way she thinks or engages in a behavior that the Worry Monster tells her not to, her worry and fear lessen, and she becomes more confident. Not only have you taught your child to tame the Worry Monster, you also have taught her to be resilient and to deal with life's adversities as they inevitably come. That's it! It really is that straightforward. While these ideas and strategies are simple to read, we all know, and must remember, that it takes a lot of courage to put them into practice.

The take-home message is that worry, fear, and anxiety can be overcome. Those feelings are not nearly so powerful when we understand that there is a Worry Monster making us feel them, and like the Wizard of Oz, he is only a pathetic bully behind a curtain. Talk to your child about how her brain works—the part that is responsible for keeping her safe and alive (the amygdala) and the part that does all of her great thinking (the frontal lobes). Tell her how the amygdala sends signals through her body so that she can survive in situations where she needs to be able to fight or run. Tell her that her worrisome and scary thoughts, given to her by the Worry Monster, are responsible for 99.9% of all of her worry and fear. Tell her that she needs to be aware of her thinking. She needs to know her thoughts—how to identify them, modify them, mold them, replace them, do jumping jacks around them until they crack, and change them into healthier thoughts. Remind your child to stay in the present. Breathe with her—deep, long breaths, in and out. Help her identify behaviors and strategies that systematically weaken the Worry Monster and promote her self-confidence and inner strength. Then help your child practice those behaviors over and over and over again.

Always remember that the Worry Monster is trying to trick us into not living to our fullest life potential. You now have the tools to help your child become a warrior, defeat the Worry Monster, and be prepared for life's many challenges. Show the Worry Monster who's boss! Send him into exile! He's no match for your team. Look at him now. You can't see him? That's because he is running scared. Reading this book has made him worried and weak. Go get him! It is time to finish him off! Best of luck on your adventure.

Suggested Reading and Resources

For Children

Crist, J. J. (2004). *What to do when you're scared and worried: A guide for kids.* Minneapolis, MN: Free Spirit.

Henke, K., & Hamilton, L. (2010). *Wemberly worried.* Pine Plains, NY: Live Oak Media.

Lester, H. (2003). *Something might happen.* Boston: Houghton Mifflin/ Walter Lorraine Books.

Maier, I. (2004). *When Lizzy was afraid of trying new things.* Washington, DC: Magination Press.

Viorst, J. (1987). *Alexander and the terrible, horrible, no good, very bad day.* New York: Aladdin.

Willems, M. (2005). *Leonardo, the terrible monster.* New York: Hyperion.

For Adolescents

Adderholdt, M., & Goldberg, J. (1999). *Perfectionism: What's bad about being too good?* Minneapolis, MN: Free Spirit.

Hipp, E. (2008). *Fighting invisible tigers: A stress management guide for teens* (3rd ed.). Minneapolis, MN: Free Spirit.

Rivero, L. (2010). *The smart teens' guide to living with intensity.* Scottsdale, AZ: Great Potential Press.

Tompkins, M. A., & Martinez, K. M. (2013). *My anxious mind: A teen's guide to managing anxiety and panic.* Washington, DC: Magination Press.

For Parents

Barlow, D. H., & Craske, M. G. (2007). *Mastery of your anxiety and panic* (4th ed.). New York: Oxford University Press.

Dalai Lama, & Cutler, H. C. (1998). *The art of happiness: A handbook for living.* New York: Riverwood Books.

Gilman, B. J., Lovecky, D. V., Kearney, K., Peters, D. B., Wasserman, J. D., Silverman, L. K.,...Rimm, S. B. (2013). *Critical issues in the identification of gifted students with co-existing disabilities: The twice-exceptional.* http://sgo.sagepub.com/content/3/3/2158244013505855.full

Greene, R. W. (2014). *The explosive child: A new approach for understanding and parenting easily frustrated, chronically inflexible children* (5th ed.). New York: HarperCollins.

Greenspon, T. S. (2002). *Freeing our families from perfectionism.* Minneapolis, MN: Free Spirit.

Kurcinka, M. S. (2006). *Raising your spirited child: A guide for parents whose child is more intense, sensitive, perceptive, persistent, and energetic* (rev. ed.). New York: HarperCollins.

Levine, M. (2012). *Teach your children well: Parenting for authentic success.* New York: HarperCollins.

Liebgold, H. (2004). *Freedom from fear: Overcoming anxiety, phobias, and panic.* New York: Kensington.

Paterson, R. J. (2000). *The assertiveness workbook: How to express your ideas and stand up for yourself at work and in relationships.* Oakland, CA: New Harbinger.

Reivich, R., & Shatté, A. (2002). *The resilience factor: 7 keys to finding your inner strength and overcoming life's hurdles.* New York: Broadway Books.

Rivero, L. (2010). *A parent's guide to gifted teens: Living with intense and creative adolescents.* Scottsdale, AZ: Great Potential Press.

Seligman, M. E. P. (1996). *The optimistic child: A proven program to safeguard children against depression and build lifelong resilience.* New York: Houghton Mifflin.

Seligman, M. E. P. (1998). *Learned optimism: How to change your mind and your life.* New York: Pocket Books.

Seligman, M. E. P. (2002). *Authentic happiness: Using the new positive psychology to realize your potential for lasting fulfillment.* New York: Free Press.

Webb, J. T., Gore, J. L, Amend, E. R., & DeVries, A. R. (2007). *A parent's guide to gifted children.* Scottsdale, AZ: Great Potential Press.

Zucker, B. (2009). *Anxiety-free kids: An interactive guide for parents and children.* Waco, TX: Prufrock Press.

Additional Resources

Taming the Monster DVD by Dan Peters, Ph.D.: www.summitcenter.us

Shrinking the Worry Monster children's books and parenting seminars by Sally F. Baird, Ph.D., R.N.: www.SallyBairdphd.com

Additional Resources for Promoting Healthy Communities

Challenge Success: www.challengesucess.org

Race to Nowhere: www.racetonowhere.com

Fostering Resilience: www.fosteringresilience.com

Mental Health America: www.mentalhealthamerica.net

Resiliency in Action: www.resiliency.com

Let's Erase the Stigma: www.lets.org

Endnotes

Acknowledgments
1   Persons, 1989
2   Zimmerman & Dickerson, 1996
3   Reivich & Shatté, 2002; Seligman, 2002

Introduction
4   National Institute of Mental Health, n.d.

Chapter 2
5   Liebgold, 1998b
6   Barlow & Craske, 2007
7   Liebgold, 2004, p. 27
8   Liebgold, 1998a, 1998b
9   Tompkins & Martinez, 2013

Chapter 3
10 Barlow & Craske, 2007
11 Most often, people who have panic attacks have to learn how to breathe by taking slow, deep breaths. The folktale remedy of breathing into a paper bag is only likely to make a panic attack worse because it increases the amount of carbon dioxide that enters the bloodstream (see Barlow & Craske, 2007).
12 Greenspon, 2002
13 Silverman, 2009
14 Greenspon, 2002
15 Adderholdt & Goldberg, 1999
16 Barlow & Craske, 2007

Chapter 4
17 Liebgold, 1998b

Chapter 5
18 Zucker, 2009
19 Liebgold, 2004
20 Barlow & Craske, 2007

Chapter 6
21 Beck, 1979; Ellis & Harper, 1979
22 Liebgold, 1998b
23 Zucker, 2009

Chapter 7
24 Kabat-Zinn, 1990
25 Dalai Lama & Cutler, 1998
26 Dalai Lama & Cutler, 1998, p. 268
27 Barlow & Craske, 2007

Chapter 8
28 Skinner, 1965
29 Liebgold, 2004
30 Liebgold, 1998b
31 Webb, Gore, Amend, & DeVries, 2007
32 Liebgold, 1998b
33 Liebgold, 2004
34 Scott, 2013
35 Adderholdt & Goldberg, 1999
36 Reivich & Shatté, 2002

Chapter 10
37 Liebgold, 1998b

Chapter 11
38 Liebgold 1998b
39 Webb et al., 2007
40 Tomkins & Martinez, 2013
41 Liebgold, 2004
42 Liebgold, 2004
43 National Sleep Foundation, n.d.
44 Knop, 2009

Chapter 12

45 "Giftedness is asynchronous development in which advanced cognitive abilities and heightened intensity combine to create inner experiences and awareness that are qualitatively different from the norm. This asynchrony increases with higher intellectual capacity. The uniqueness of the gifted renders them vulnerable and requires modifications in parenting, teaching and counseling in order for them to develop optimally" (Columbus Group, 1991).

46 Webb et al., 2007

47 Daniels & Piechowski, 2009

48 For more information and practical advice, parents are encouraged to look at books like *A Parent's Guide to Gifted Children* (Webb et al., 2007), *The Gifted Kids' Survival Guide* (Galbraith, 2009), and *The Smart Teen's Guide to Living with Intensity* (Rivero, 2010).

49 Gilman et al., 2013

References

Adderholdt, M., & Goldberg, J. (1999). *Perfectionism: What's bad about being too good?* Minneapolis, MN: Free Spirit.

Barlow, D. H., & Craske, M. G. (2007). *Mastery of your anxiety and panic* (4th ed.). New York: Oxford University Press.

Beck, A. T. (1979). *Cognitive therapy and the emotional disorders.* New York: Penguin.

Columbus Group. (1991). Unpublished transcript of the meeting of the Columbus Group, Columbus, OH.

Dalai Lama, & Cutler, H. C. (1998). *The art of happiness: A handbook for living.* New York: Riverwood Books.

Daniels, S., & Piechowski, M. M. (Eds.). (2009). *Living with intensity: Understanding the sensitivity, excitability, and emotional development of gifted children, adolescents, and adults.* Scottsdale, AZ: Great Potential Press.

Ellis, A., & Harper, R. A. (1979). *A guide to rational living* (3rd ed.). North Hollywood, CA: Wilshire Books.

Galbraith, J. (2009). *The gifted kids' survival guide.* Minneapolis, MN: Free Spirit.

Gilman, B. J., Lovecky, D. V., Kearney, K., Peters, D. B., Wasserman, J. D., Silverman, L. K.,...Rimm, S. B. (2013). *Critical issues in the identification of gifted students with co-existing disabilities: The twice-exceptional.* Retrieved from http://sgo.sagepub.com/content/3/3/2158244013505855.full

Greenspon, T. S. (2002). *Freeing our families from perfectionism.* Minneapolis, MN: Free Spirit.

Kabat-Zinn, J. (1990). *Full catastrophe living.* New York: Dell.

Knop, N. (2009). *Sleep to learn: Recent research.* California Association of Independent Schools (CAIS) faculty newsletter. Retrieved from www.caisca.org/page/22434_Archived_Publications.asp

Liebgold, H. (1998a). *Children's curing anxiety, phobias, shyness and obsessive compulsive disorders: The phobease way* (5th ed.). Retrieved from www.angelnet.com

Liebgold, H. (1998b). *Curing anxiety, phobias, shyness and obsessive compulsive disorders: The phobease way* (5th ed.). Retrieved from www.angelnet.com

Liebgold, H. (2004). *Freedom from fear: Overcoming anxiety, phobias, and panic.* New York: Kensington.

National Institute of Mental Health. (n.d.). *What is anxiety disorder?* Retrieved from www.nimh.nih.gov/health/topics/anxiety-disorders/index.shtml#part4

National Sleep Foundation. (n.d.). *Children and sleep/Teens and sleep.* Retrieved from www.sleepfoundation.org/article/sleep-topics/children-and-sleep; www.sleepfoundation.org/article/sleep-topics/teens-and-sleep

Persons, J. B. (1989). *Cognitive therapy in practice: A case formulation approach.* New York: W.W. Norton & Co.

Reivich, K., & Shatté, A. (2002). *The resilience factor: 7 keys to finding your inner strength and overcoming life's hurdles.* New York: Broadway Books.

Rivero, L. (2010). *The smart teens' guide to living with intensity.* Scottsdale, AZ: Great Potential Press.

Scott, E. (2013). *The stress management and health benefits of laughter.* Retrieved from http://stress.about.com/od/stresshealth/a/laughter.htm

Seligman. M. E. P. (2002). *Authentic happiness: Using the new positive psychology to realize your potential for lasting fulfillment.* New York: Free Press.

Silverman, L. K. (2009). Petunias, perfectionism, and level of development. In S. Daniels & M. M. Piechowski (Eds.), *Living with intensity Understanding the sensitivity, excitability, and emotional development of gifted children, adolescents, and adults.* Scottsdale, AZ: Great Potential Press.

Skinner, B. F. (1965). *Science and human behavior.* New York: Free Press.

Tompkins, M. A., & Martinez, K. M. (2013). *My anxious mind: A teen's guide to managing anxiety and panic.* Washington, DC: Magination Press.

Webb, J. T., Gore, J. L., Amend, E. R., & DeVries, A. R. (2007). *A parent's guide to gifted children.* Scottsdale, AZ: Great Potential Press.

Zimmerman, J. L., & Dickerson, V. C. (1996). *If problems talked: Narrative therapy in action.* New York: Guilfold Press.

Zucker, B. (2009). *Anxiety-free kids: An interactive guide for parents and children.* Waco, TX: Prufrock Press.

Index

2e. *See* twice-exceptional

adrenaline, 22-3, 27, 42, 45, 50-2, 65, 86, 123, 134, 150

agoraphobia, 31-2

all or nothing thinking, 54

amygdala, 20-3, 27, 44, 47-8, 50-2, 64-5, 70, 73, 76, 81, 123, 133-4, 140, 169
  See also emotional brain

"And then what?" 71-2, 74

anorexia, 38

anticipatory anxiety, 100

anxiety attacks, 30-2, 82, 110
  See also panic attacks

anxiety (definition), 19

Asperger's Disorder, 159

asynchronous development, 156, 160, 177

Attention Deficit/Hyperactivity Disorder (ADHD), 158, 160-1

attentional disorders, 158-60

avoidance, 31-2, 36, 43-6, 95, 110

baby steps, 87-90, 93, 110, 112, 137, 140, 142, 146

Barlow, David, 58

behavioral rehearsal, 94-6

behaviorism, 85

Body Dysmorphic Disorder, 38

breathing techniques, 81-4, 175

bribe, 109

bulimia, 38

catastrophizing, 54, 57, 72

Central Auditory Processing Disorder (CAPD), 159

cognition, 47

cognitive behavior therapy (CBT), 85-7, 126, 151-2

cognitive model of anxiety, 47-8

Craske, Michelle, 58

Dabrowski, Kazimierz, 157

Dalai Lama, 75-6

depression, 35, 63, 75-6, 159

diet, 149-50, 153

distraction, 97, 120, 126, 140-1, 147-8, 161, 163

dysgraphia, 2, 159

dyslexia, 2, 159

eating disorders, 38-9

emotional brain, 26-7, 44, 51, 64, 123, 133
  See also amygdala

exercise, 141, 149-50, 153-4

exposure, 87, 91, 94

expectant praise, 91

fake it to make it, 99-100

fight or flight response, 6, 20, 23, 27, 44, 52, 117-18, 123-4, 127, 134, 168

filtering, 54-5

food allergies, 149

Freedom from Fear, 95

frontal lobes (of the brain), 47, 51, 64, 169
  See also thinking brain

Full Catastrophe Living, 75

generalized anxiety, 30
giftedness, 33, 36, 155-8, 160-1, 163
goal vaulting, 37
hypoglycemia, 149
incentives/incentivizing, 99, 109-10,
    138, 145
Kabat-Zinn, Jon, 75
King Kong, 79
learning disorders, 158-60
Liebgold, Howard, xi-xiii, 23, 50, 95, 145
Little Engine that Could, The, 68-9
magnifying, 55, 57, 72
medication, 152-3
mental health professional/counselor/
    therapist, 7, 40, 151-3, 160
mind reading, 56
mindfulness, 75, 81, 83
motivation, 93, 104, 109, 112-13, 119,
    121, 139, 142, 146, 152-3, 167
Murray, Bill, 87
National Sleep Foundation, 150
negative reinforcement, 109
Nietzsche, Friedrich, 150
Obsessive-Compulsive Disorder
    (OCD)/OCD Monster, 32-3, 96-8,
    112, 117-22, 127-30, 132, 142, 152
occupational therapist, 160
overexcitabilities, 157-8, 162
overgeneralizing, 56-7
panic attacks, 30-1, 41, 125, 175
    See also anxiety attacks
pediatrician, 152
perfectionism/Perfectionism Monster,
    3-4, 13, 36-9, 102-8, 112, 129-30,
    132, 142, 161
personalizing, 56
Phobease, xi, 50
pleasure predicting, 100-2
positive reinforcement, 109
Post-Traumatic Stress Disorder (PTSD),
    34-5
prescribing failure, 103-4
probability overestimation, 57
processing disorders, 158-60
procrastination, 105
professional help (mental health). See
    mental health professional
psychiatrist, child, 152

reinforcement, 31, 44, 85, 97, 109-10,
    112-13, 126, 133, 139, 146, 154
    See also negative reinforcement,
    positive reinforcement
Reivich, Karen, 111
resilience, 5, 111-12, 168
response inhibition, 96-9, 117, 119-20,
    128
rewards, 99, 109-10, 121, 139, 142
risk taking. See taking a risk
role model, 7, 167
scare ratings, 92, 94, 113, 119, 136
scare steps, 118-19, 139
selective attention, 55
self-knowledge, 101
self-management, 152
self-talk, 68-70, 74, 91, 134, 140, 168
Sensory Integration Disorder (SID)/
    Sensory Processing Disorder (SPD),
    159
separation anxiety, 35-6
Shatté, Andrew, 111
"shoulds," 55-6
sleep, 43, 116-17, 150-1, 153-4
social phobia, 34
specific phobia, 33-4, 123
stinking thinking, 53, 79, 97
success ladders, 87, 91-4, 113, 118-19,
    121, 137, 139, 145-6
survival response, 20-6, 67, 81-2, 91,
    110, 112, 127, 134, 141
systematic desensitization, 87, 91, 93-4
taking a risk, 37, 102-3
thinking brain, 26-7, 44, 51, 64, 70, 78,
    110, 123, 133
    See also frontal lobes
thinking errors, 53, 58-60, 64-5, 72, 138
tics, 43
toolbox, 6, 118, 120-2, 130-3, 140-1,
    148, 153
twice-exceptional (2e), 160-1
What about Bob?, 87
"What if...?" 57-8
"What will people think...?" 57-8
Wizard of Oz, The, 14-15, 136, 169
worry box, 71, 74, 78, 117, 120, 141
worry time, 70-1, 74, 117, 120, 141
worst-case scenarios, 72-4, 112

About the Author

Dan Peters, Ph.D., is a licensed psychologist who has devoted his career to the assessment and treatment of children, adolescents, and families, specializing in those who are gifted, creative, and twice-exceptional (2e). As a parent of three children, he understands the daily challenges of raising children in today's world, as well as the importance of teaching them coping skills, problem solving, and resilience. He is passionate about creating healthy communities by helping parents and teachers engage children in the classroom, at home, and in life so that they can realize their full potential.

Dr. Peters is co-founder and Executive Director of the Summit Center, where he is available for consultation. He serves on the California Association for the Gifted (CAG) Advisory Board, the Supporting Emotional Needs of the Gifted (SENG) Editorial Board, the Advisory Board for the 2e Center for Research and Professional Development at Bridges Academy, and as Co-Chair of the Assessments of Giftedness Special Interest Group of the National Association for Gifted Children (NAGC). He speaks regularly at state and national conferences on a variety of gifted, learning, and parenting topics, including how to overcome worry and anxiety. Dr. Peters is co-author (with Dr. Susan Daniels) of *Raising Creative Kids* (Great Potential Press, 2013), as well as many articles on topics related to parenting, giftedness, twice-exceptionality, dyslexia, and anxiety. He is also co-founder of Camp Summit, a sleep-over summer camp for gifted youth. He lives in Northern California with his wife and three children.

CPSIA information can be obtained
at www.ICGtesting.com
Printed in the USA
BVHW081102120919
558278BV00009B/312/P

9 781935 067238